TOTAL
Literacy
TECHNIQUES

**TOOLS TO HELP STUDENTS ANALYZE
LITERATURE AND INFORMATIONAL TEXTS**

ASCD MEMBER BOOK

Many ASCD members received this book as a
member benefit upon its initial release.

Learn more at: **www.ascd.org/memberbooks**

TOTAL Literacy TECHNIQUES

TOOLS TO HELP STUDENTS ANALYZE LITERATURE AND INFORMATIONAL TEXTS

Pérsida Himmele / William Himmele / with Keely Potter

ASCD® Alexandria, VA USA

1703 N. Beauregard St. • Alexandria, VA 22311-1714 USA
Phone: 800-933-2723 or 703-578-9600 • Fax: 703-575-5400
Website: www.ascd.org • E-mail: member@ascd.org
Author guidelines: www.ascd.org/write

Gene R. Carter, *Executive Director;* Richard Papale, *Acting Chief Program Development Officer;* Stefani Roth, *Interim Publisher;* Julie Houtz, *Director, Book Editing & Production;* Deborah Siegel, *Editor;* Louise Bova, *Senior Graphic Designer;* Mike Kalyan, *Manager, Production Services;* Keith Demmons, *Production Designer;* Kyle Steichen, *Production Specialist*

PAPERBACK ISBN: 978-1-4166-1883-6   ASCD product #114009

Quantity discounts: 10–49, 10%; 50+, 15%; 1,000+, special discounts (e-mail program-team@ascd.org or call 800-933-2723, ext. 5773, or 703-575-5773). Also available in e-book formats. For desk copies, go to www.ascd.org/deskcopy.

ASCD Member Book No. FY14-08B. ASCD Member Books mail to Premium (P), Select (S), and Institutional Plus (I+) members on this schedule: Jan, PSI+; Feb, P; Apr, PSI+; May, P; Jul, PSI+; Aug, P; Sep, PSI+; Nov, PSI+; Dec, P. For current details on membership, see www.ascd.org/membership.

Library of Congress Cataloging-in-Publication Data

Himmele, Pérsida.
   Total literacy techniques : tools to help students analyze literature and informational texts / Persida Himmele and William Himmele ; with Keely Potter.
      pages cm
   Includes bibliographical references and index.
   ISBN 978-1-4166-1883-6 (pbk. : alk. paper) 1. Reading. 2. Language arts. I. Himmele, William. II. Potter, Keely. III. Title.
   LB1050.H55 2014
   372.6--dc23
                                                2014010126

23 22 21 20 19 18 17 16 15 14   1 2 3 4 5 6 7 8 9 10 11 12

TOTAL Literacy Techniques

Tools to Help Students Analyze Literature and Informational Texts

Acknowledgments

We'd like to express our deep appreciation to the many people who collaborated with us on this writing project. First and foremost, we'd like to thank our ASCD Acquisitions Editor, Stefani Roth, and our Project Manager, Deborah Siegel. Their knowledgeable and discerning eyes were very helpful to us in improving the quality of this work.

We'd also like to thank Keely Potter's current and former 5th through 8th grade students whose insights kept us grounded, and her building administrator, Tammy Woolbright, whose support and insights were very helpful in our writing of this book.

Several other educators also contributed to this book in very meaningful ways. We'd like to thank Conestoga Valley School District and the following contributors and their students: Curricular Leader Michelle Trasborg, and the following educators and educational leaders: Colette Barnett, Katie Fake, Debbie Denlinger, Laura Gingrich, Gina Bray, Melanie Upton, Susan Grammer, Nicole Reinking, Victoria Henderson, Ramón Rivera, Dan Daneker, Superintendent Dr. Gerald Huesken, and administrator Dr. Kelly Cartwright.

We'd also like to thank Assistant Superintendent Margie Sharp at Avon Grove School District, whom we deeply admire and who has been gracious in sharing her insights with us. Amazing educators from neighboring districts whom we'd like to thank include Liz Lubeskie and Matt Baker from Manheim Central School District; Brandon Bailey, from Central York School District; David Vega from South Western School District; Carmen Rowe, Georgia Saldaña Jones, Susan Hagel, Krista Grimm, and Principals Arthur Paynter and Jackie Martin-Hair from the School District of Lancaster; Joanne Williard from Lampeter Strasburg School District; Director Joe Barlow of Jackson County Schools in Tennessee; Andrea

Adams from Manheim Township School District; and Jacquelyn Neudorf and Rowland Hayward from Manitoba, Canada.

We'd also like to thank our colleagues and literature gurus Dr. Leslie Colabucci and Dr. Jennifer Shettel who contributed the appendix, and teacher candidate Christine Kile, who found great research for us to review. We'd also like to thank the Millersville University Sabbatical Committee for granting us the time to gather resources toward this project. And we appreciate the many students who graciously participated through the sharing of their thoughts. Finally, we'd like to thank our Heavenly Father, the giver of language, cognition, and peace.

Introduction: Tools for Engaging Thinkers, Readers, and Writers

In today's educational landscape, it's easy to get caught up in the everyday demands of checklists and isolated skill sets. It's easy to lose sight of the interconnectedness of the development of academic language, higher-order thinking, reading, writing, and the power of well-planned text-based classroom interactions. The goal of this text is to provide a context for reevaluating that interconnectedness as a more complete picture in an attempt to engage students as thinkers, readers, and writers. In essence, this text is about helping students celebrate words and the potential power that well-chosen words can carry. In a practical sense, it aims to provide teachers with more than 50 tools and techniques for addressing the following questions:

- How might we foster environments and plan lessons aimed at growing academic language using what research tells us works?
- How might we help students explicitly and implicitly develop and monitor their ability to think using higher-order thinking as they engage with text?
- How might we ensure that students are not just consumers of powerful words but producers of powerful words?
- How might we frame our interactions with text so that all children provide evidence of processing using higher-order thinking via well-planned peer interactions?
- How might we support students so that they are able not only to cite text-based evidence but also to coherently interpret its relevance for the reader?

In our previous book, *Total Participation Techniques: Making Every Student an Active Learner*, we used the term *total* to refer to the percentage of students actively participating and cognitively engaged with the content of the lessons. This text does include a chapter on text-based *Total Participation Techniques* (see Chapter 6) however, in this text we use the term *total* to refer to the interconnectedness of the roles of deeper thinking processes, academic language development, peer interactions, and reading and writing. Each of these roles enhances overall literacy development in a way that provides students with the type of success that is long-term and sustainable. This book provides a more complete picture of literacy as a pathway to whole-child development that embeds social and cognitive growth processes.

Through teacher-tested tools and student voices, we provide tools and techniques for helping students comprehend, analyze, discuss, and create text that enhances students' growth as reflective learners. Throughout much of this book, we will introduce you to students who reflect on their literary practices and journeys. We hope that you find these tools and techniques, as well as the student and teacher insights, to be helpful in supporting your students in their development as lifelong, independent, and critical thinkers, readers, and writers.

1

Growing Academic Language: Building Foundations for Academic Literacy

Perhaps the story in the book is just the lid on a pan: It always stays the same, but underneath there's a whole world that goes on.
—Inkheart (Funke, 2003, p. 1470)

Have you ever been lost in a really good book? So lost you didn't even notice the type of vocabulary that the author used to draw you in, compelling you to read on well into the night, even though you should have gone to sleep long ago? Many students can't experience the pleasure of being lost in a good book because of the intense focus that is necessary for them to successfully decode their way through the text. The frustration of repeatedly stumbling as they make their way through text will preclude any enjoyment students experience from reading. And aside from the misfortune of missing out on a great literary experience, this phenomenon has linguistic and academic implications that can negatively affect students' academic growth throughout their entire academic careers.

In fact, without the prerequisite ingredients needed to get lost in a good book, we can forget all about the lofty goals we hope to accomplish through more rigorous and well-meaning standards that are related to students independently and critically reading grade-level literature and informational texts. Being able to do that still requires simple comprehension as a precursor to analysis and to using other higher-order thinking skills exercised in processing what was read.

To help many students make the crossover into deep reading will require a strategic scaffolding of students' interactions with text, student-to-student interactions around text, and pointed support in effectively writing about the text. It will also require our carefully setting the stage for students to critically interpret what they read within the text. If we're serious about providing all students with meaningful access to all aspects of the curricula, it's going to take a well-thought-out game plan that is informed by who the students are, where they are, and what they'll need. We won't be able to get there if we ignore the necessary scaffolds.

Navigating the Language of the Text

There is a profound difference between the language we speak and the language we read. The language in books is often perfectly crafted to convey precise meanings. It is typically more grammatically complex than spoken language. And for most nonillustrated chapter books, it is void of any supports that are not solely linguistic. There is also quite a difference between the language that students read in fictional stories and the type of language that they come across in informational text. Unlike stories, informational text doesn't reward readers with the promise of a good ending to conclude a narrative that has drawn them in or captivated them for several hours. According to 7th grader Selena, "I haven't been as successful with nonfiction, because there's nothing to enjoy in it." And unlike spoken words, the language in informational texts is not accompanied by hand gestures, facial expressions, and situational contexts that support the recipients' understandings. Informational text has a different structure to it. In most cases, all that readers have to hang their comprehension on is words put together in unfamiliar patterns and structures that deal with technical, usually unfamiliar, material that will often fail to pique students' interests.

According to Nagy and Townsend (2012), among the unique challenges that academic language presents are complexities like grammatical metaphor and informational density. Grammatical metaphor refers to phrases that are used in contexts that do not apply to their typical meanings—for example, the term *boils down to*. Adults familiar with this term may not even notice that it could be a source of confusion for students. Students, on the other hand, may be left wondering how anything they are reading has to do with boiling liquids.

Academic language also contains morphologically complex words and a high degree of technicality and abstractness. It packs all of these complexities into meaningfully dense sentences that are structurally complicated and that are unlike spoken language. For example, they contain more ideas using fewer words, requiring more focus and more rereadings on the part of the reader. The more difficult the words and the more complex the structures, the more experiences students will need with those words, and the more motivation they'll need to make sense of what they read. While 7th grader Hayley enjoys reading fiction, she finds nonfiction much more of a challenge. "When I read nonfiction, it doesn't always make that much sense. I don't really understand it. I don't understand how they word things." In preparing students to succeed with informational texts, we will need to address approaches to helping students understand the academic language that can so often cause them to stumble.

The Vocabulary Gap

The National Assessment of Educational Progress (NAEP) results point to a persistent and growing vocabulary gap by socioeconomic status as well as by race and ethnicity (National Center for Education Statistics [NCES], 2012). School-like experiences at home divide children long before they actually enter school. We know that children who are exposed to more sophisticated school-like or academic caretaker speech end up having a larger school-like vocabulary (Hoff, 2003; Roberts & Kaiser, 2011; Weizman & Snow, 2001). This is true even when the increase in the amount of exposure to linguistically and cognitively complex speech is relatively small. Ruston and Schwanenflugel (2010) found that a twice-weekly 25-minute intervention of exposure to more sophisticated academic language was followed by an increase in the complexity of expressive vocabulary for students in the study's experimental group. We also know that students who have experienced read-alouds (stories read to children) have a larger academic vocabulary than their peers who have not participated in read-aloud experiences (Elley & Mangubhai, 1983; Meehan, 1999; Roberts, 2008; Sénéchal & LeFevre, 2002; Sharif, Ozuah, Dinkevich, & Muklvihill, 2003).

We acquire language through experiencing it in contexts we understand. Books provide that comprehensible linguistic experience. So, not surprisingly, there is strong evidence of a positive link between vocabulary development and the read-aloud experience. Subsequently, students with stronger early language development learn to read more quickly and develop better reading comprehension (Biemiller, 2003; Dickinson & Porche, 2011; Rodriguez & Tamis-LeMonda, 2011; Shany & Biemiller, 1995, 2010). In short, exposure to academic language in contextually rich environments, such as the read-aloud experience and sophisticated caretaker speech, has a direct influence on academic vocabulary growth, which in turn affects reading development.

It's Not Just About Language

If it were just a matter of some students having a different kind of speech or fancier academic speech than others, the growing vocabulary gap outlined in the NAEP study might not matter as much. But the impact of the vocabulary gap affects every aspect of schooling that is dependent upon reading ability. Additionally, timing matters. Stanovich's (1986) synthesis of reading studies points to evidence of a snowball effect that occurs both for those who develop literacy skills early and for those who develop them later. This phenomenon is often referred to as the "Matthew effect" in reference to a Bible story found in Matthew 25:14–30. The story contrasts a wise and a foolish investor. It concludes, "For whoever has will be given more, and they will have an abundance. Whoever does not have, even what they have will be taken from them." In essence, the Matthew effect points to the phenomenon of the rich getting richer and the poor getting poorer. The Matthew effect has a substantial impact on all areas of literacy development and, subsequently, academic achievement. Those who develop literacy skills sooner continue to progress, while those who develop them later continue to fall behind (Biemiller & Slonim, 2001).

Allow us to focus on how the Matthew effect works when it comes to vocabulary growth. Isabel Beck, a well-known author and researcher, has written extensively about vocabulary development, but it's this personal account of her own experience with vocabulary that we feel best describes how children use selective attention to tune in and out of conversations that contain unfamiliar words, and the resulting snowball effect that vocabulary growth has on additional vocabulary growth.

> I remember learning the word *earnest*; it was in the fourth grade and a character had been described as earnest. . . At about the time I learned about earnest, I began to notice that other people were catching on to it, too. I started noticing the word in newspapers and even overheard it in a conversation. It was amazing to me that I was somehow a part of a group of people across the country who had simultaneously discovered the word earnest! (Beck, McKeown, & Kucan, 2002, p. vii)

What we like about this personal account is the way it cleanly portrays how learning new words opens up new conversations to us. The conversations that Beck had heard prior to her learning the word *earnest* still existed. She had simply tuned them out. Our students do that, too. When they learn new words, that conversation then opens up other new words embedded within conversations that would have otherwise been tuned out. The context of these once inaccessible conversations is now clearer because of new known words, and additional words can be picked up based on their being embedded within that meaningful context. In other words, the more vocabulary children know, the more vocabulary they'll learn. The less vocabulary they know, the less vocabulary they'll learn. According to Biemiller, "unfortunately, slower learners do not 'catch up.' If we could avoid the growing vocabulary gap during kindergarten to grade two, and possibly fill in some words already missing at the beginning of kindergarten, reading comprehension, perhaps, could be improved" (2003, p. 328). Rather than taking lack of academic vocabulary development as a given and unchangeable circumstance, the classroom itself needs to be a place where all students are immersed in opportunities to soak in comprehensible academic language in ways that can help bridge that vocabulary gap. In other words, academic language development needs to be an academic priority in schools for students of all ages.

The *Blah* Words

Just how much of an impact does the lack of academic language have on a student's comprehension of informational texts? When we asked a particularly well-read 8th grader what she found confusing about informational text, she guided us to this chapter in her history book, which she indicated was one example of the many that left her with a frustrating lack of understanding. A sample paragraph reads as follows:

> Under the terms of the Compromise, popular sovereignty would be used to decide the question of slavery in the rest of the Mexican Cession. People in the states created from that territory would vote whether to be a free state or a slave state when they requested admission to the Union. Also, in return for agreeing to outlaw the slave trade in Washington D.C., southerners got a tough new fugitive slave law. (Davidson & Stoff, 2007, p. 486)

We asked her to read the paragraph out loud, substituting the word *blah* when she got to a word she didn't understand. This process gave us a better feel for how she understood this paragraph and provides insight into the importance of particular words for understanding the paragraph.

> Under the terms of the *Blah,* popular *blah* would be used to decide the question of slavery in the rest of the Mexican *Blah.* People in the states created from that territory would vote whether to be a free state or a slave state when they requested admission to the Union. Also, in return for agreeing to outlaw the slave trade in Washington D.C., southerners got a tough new *blah* slave law.

These same words, represented by *blah*, were unknown to another boy who also unknowingly struggled with the word *admission* in the phrase "admission to the Union." The original sentence reads, "People in the states created from that territory would vote whether to be a free state or a slave state when they requested admission to the Union." Knowing the word *admission* in the contexts of movie theaters and amusement parks, he erroneously interpreted the sentence to mean the following: "I understand that they need a ticket to get into the Union. So these people probably want to leave their states to go and move to the Union." He could not understand the sentences containing the *blah* words, and because of his lack of exposure to words in different contexts, he also misunderstood the only sentence that contained no *blah* words. We're not sure which is worse: not knowing what something means, or not knowing that you don't know what something means. Clearly, we will not be able to reach our goal of helping students independently and critically read grade-level literature and informational texts if we do not also address the hurdles associated with acquiring academic language. Our classrooms need to become places that foster academic language growth both implicitly and explicitly. By implicit language growth, we mean that students acquire understandings of these words and structures based on a comprehensible context. By explicit language growth, we mean that the teaching of academic vocabulary and language is spelled out and consciously addressed for and by students.

What Are We Really Asking of Students?

While the goal of preparing students to be able to independently and critically read grade-level literature and informational texts seems like a simple set of expectations, it entails a whole series of skill sets and a whole lot of experiences with texts. In addition to that, it must be addressed within the context of child development and the practical context of everyday schools within everyday realities. What is reasonable to expect of children at certain ages? What is most important to develop at certain ages? What about struggling readers? What about reluctant readers? What about students with minimal exposure to the type of academic language found in informational texts? What about English language learners? What about students who have learning disabilities? Where do we begin? When it comes to more rigorous expectations for all students, these are the questions that teachers are asking. While exploring the answers to these questions will take a great deal of teacher intuition, we do know that a good place to begin is with a conscious and strategic effort toward building the academic language of all students, so that they can make sense of what they read.

Academic Vocabulary Versus Academic Language

Building students' academic language involves more than just racking up sophisticated words. Academic language is complicated. We want to make a distinction between academic vocabulary and academic language. For the purposes of this text, we define academic vocabulary as referring to non-content–specific academic words that would be considered low-frequency words but are high-utility words for the audience being discussed. In other words, they are "fancy" words, but not ridiculously so. They are low-frequency words, because they are typically not spoken by students in conversational contexts. But they are somewhat high-utility words because we can be confident that students will encounter these words again in their future readings. For example, there is very little point in focusing time and energy on a vocabulary word like *esurient* if the next time we can expect students to come across this word is when they are 40, if at all. Academic vocabulary refers to words like *impending* and *crisis* that realistically may be encountered in texts. Academic language, on the other hand, refers to the whole package of how words are put together to create meaningful cognitively complex messages. For example, consider this sentence written by 9th grader Kinsey: "Books carry truth, whether that truth be light or dark; and by reading these books, we build our hearts out of words." Intense, no? Yet the sentence uses only nonacademic high-frequency words for a 9th grader. But, because of the complexity of how the words are put together to create imagery and to cause readers to think deeply about the statements she makes, we would characterize this sentence as making use of academic language.

So, academic language is not just words; it also refers to the way words are manipulated to carry cognitively complex messages. Ninth grader Alison addresses this skill when she described what she loved most about a favorite book. According to Alison, "One of the best things about the book for me was that it was a challenge. There were new vocabulary words, of course. There were also words and phrases put together in ways I would have never thought of."

The distinction between academic language and academic vocabulary is an important one, because throughout this book we will use samples of text and student work that use academic language but not necessarily academic vocabulary. Both Kinsey and Alison are referring to beautiful words found within the pages of literature. However, the academic language found in informational texts may not be so much beautiful as it is baffling. For example, a sentence like "Likewise, investigators found culpability on the part of the ship's crew, in that the ratio of life jackets to passengers was negligently low" may cause readers to need to double back and reread. Our goal is to help students be able not only to read and comprehend academic vocabulary and language found in literature and informational texts, but also to analyze and re-create academic language in effective ways toward meeting their academic goals. In order to do that, we will need to address the topic of academic language, both explicitly and implicitly. We will need to immerse students in language that, in 9th grader Kinsey's words, "I connect to, or that I think hold brilliance, such as metaphors, symbolic meanings or things that make me wish that I had come up with them."

Where Is Academic Language Found?

Where can teachers find academic vocabulary? And, where does academic language come from? If we view academic vocabulary as more than just content-area-specific words, we can more clearly understand what it is in content reading that stumps children, especially those with fewer reading experiences. For the most part, content-area-specific words such as *colony*, *Puritan,* and *Pilgrim* are introduced and taught to children at about the same times in their schooling careers. These content-specific words are not typically spoken by 4th graders, for example, on a playground. As a result, the teacher is often alert to the fact that all of the students will need to be given an overview of these words at some point prior to or within the lesson. The non-content-specific vocabulary is another matter altogether. Words like *conscientious*, *presume*, *resemble*, and the thousands of other words that often stump readers may never directly be taught in school.

These same words are not at all likely to be experienced in everyday conversations on the playground with peers, or even with teachers. But for some students, repeated prior exposure to these words in the form of independent reading and read-aloud experiences have provided a boost to comprehension, so that whether or not students are actually ready to use these words in their own speech, they are more likely to comprehend them when they see these words in the context of an academic text. This is less likely to be the case for students who have had fewer independent reading or read-aloud experiences (Cunningham & Stanovich, 2001). While the content-specific vocabulary is generally introduced to all students at the same time by the teacher who is teaching in that specific content area, non-content-specific vocabulary is subject to the literary experiences and to the exposure that each student has had to words in books and through sophisticated conversations with the adults in their lives.

Literature as an Indispensable Component

Quite a bit happens when students get lost in a good book. Beyond just providing an enjoyable literary experience, both fiction and nonfiction can be excellent sources of academic language. The types of words that authors use to add texture and imagery to stories are often the same types of words that inhibit students' comprehension of content-based academic texts. Certain types of words are harder to learn than others. Concrete nouns, for example, are easier to acquire than adjectives and adverbs (Elley, 1989). But it's the adjectives and adverbs that add to the unique attributes of the characters, the setting, and the plot. In stories, these words become gradually understood through repeated exposure within meaningful contexts. Informational texts have less time to present a meaningful context. They are often brief and extremely focused in their intent. Informational texts are also loaded with the types of words that students would consider to be difficult words. But while great stories allow students to hang comprehension of more difficult unknown words on known words and the contexts surrounding them, informational texts rarely are able to do that.

In stories, the context itself begins to paint a picture for students that allows readers to fill in the blanks that would normally be left by unknown words. An informational text that makes use of words like *conscientious*, *resemble*, *presume*, *region*, and *rare* might leave 4th graders with comprehension glitches that inhibit student understandings. However, consider the language that is plentiful in books like *The Mysterious Benedict Society and the Perilous Journey* by Trenton Lee Stewart (2008). It uses the words *conscientious*, *resemble*, *presume*, *region*, and *rare*, along with other words and sentence structures that are not typical in everyday conversation.

> Reynie's brow wrinkled. That conscientious goat was not the first unusual thing he'd seen this morning. He was reminded of something else—something curious to which, in his excitement, he hadn't given much thought until now. Reynie shaded his eyes and searched the sky. There, circling quite low overhead, was the falcon he had noticed earlier. He could just make out its facial markings, which resembled a black cap and long black sideburns. Reynie didn't presume to know much about birds (though in fact he knew more than most people), but he felt sure that this was a peregrine falcon—and in this region, at this time of year, peregrine falcons were very rare indeed. (Stewart, 2008, pp. 3–4)

Within this paragraph alone, students are exposed to non-content-specific academic words not typically spoken by 4th graders to 4th graders, yet a child independently reading this book or experiencing this book as a read-aloud would be introduced to these words within a context that is enjoyable as well as comprehensible. In contrast, an informational text using the same academic words would likely leave students flustered, in large part due to its brevity and lack of contextually rich imagery. Increased exposure to literature that is rich in academic vocabulary, like the book noted above, can support students by providing contextually meaningful repeated exposure to the type of academic language that they will eventually find embedded throughout informational texts. Seventh grader Jaycie said it best when discussing her ability to read through a narrative chapter book that contained quite a bit of complex vocabulary: "There were some difficult vocabulary words, but I thought that the way the author put some context clues around it made it easy to understand. And I've noticed that I've grown to use those words a lot more than I did."

Exposure to vocabulary within the meaningful contexts of leisure reading and read-alouds is an important backdrop to growing academic language. Nagy, Herman, and Anderson (1985) found that students who had been exposed to passages that contained certain complex target vocabulary scored better on tests containing the target vocabulary that had appeared in the passages, even though the words had never been explicitly taught. Elley and Mangubhai (1983) found that children who were in a storybook-based program progressed in reading and listening comprehension at twice the rate of students learning language through a more traditional non-reading-based program. The growth not only was sustained, but continued to outpace the language growth made by students in the control group. Elley's later studies confirmed his earlier findings. Vocabulary acquisition was accelerated significantly through high-interest reading and the read-aloud experience (1989, 1991, 2000). This was true whether or not the readings were accompanied by teacher explanations of new vocabulary. Pairing the read-aloud experiences with timely teacher explanations led to even greater vocabulary growth (Elley, 1989). The advantages of teaching vocabulary implicitly through leisure reading as compared to through direct instruction was one of the components of language acquisition examined by Stephen Krashen in his book *The Power of Reading* (2004). In his review of numerous reading studies, Krashen makes a strong case for leisure reading as the best way to acquire vocabulary. According to Krashen, "teaching vocabulary lists is not efficient. Time is better spent in reading" (p.19). Krashen's statement takes on greater significance when we evaluate the full complexity of academic language and not just academic vocabulary.

Consider the following reading conference interview with 8th grader Gabriela, who was asked to select an excerpt to share, along with a favorite line (underlined). Notice the amount of language that she is able to understand from what is implied. Notice how she correctly determines the meaning of the word *unobtrusive* using contextual clues. Also notice that she is able to analyze the author's craft and make inferences with regard to the purpose of the particular style employed by the author in order to achieve a specific tone. Chapter 4 contains a suggested list of these and other questions to ask during a reading conference (see Figure 4.2).

Gabriela's chosen excerpt, with her favorite sentence underlined:

> Hobbits are an unobtrusive but very ancient people, more
> numerous formerly than they are today; for they love peace

and quiet and good tilled earth: a well-ordered and well-farmed countryside was their favorite haunt. <u>They do not and did not understand or like machines more complicated than a forge-bellows, a water-mill, or a hand-loom, though they were skillful with tools.</u> Even in ancient days they were, as a rule, shy of "the Big Folk," as they call us, and now they avoid us with dismay and are becoming hard to find. (J. R. R. Tolkien, *The Fellowship of the Ring,* p. 1)

Interviewer: Tell me about the language he used in the excerpt.

Gabriela: I didn't understand what a forge-bellows or a hand-loom was, but they were obviously tools that they used in the olden days. But, I liked it because it's so specific, it's ridiculous. It's obviously saying that they are a simplistic people. I also like how he said, "and they were shy of the Big Folk." I thought that was kind of funny, just because, it was so specific and it makes them seem so ridiculous.

Interviewer: What do you notice about what the author is doing with language?

Gabriela: He's making it so real, like when you would use that kind of language, you'd be talking about American history, or something more real. And it's all this useless information that doesn't pertain to the book at all, but it helps the reader to believe that it's a real world and that it's got an actual history, and it's not just a story. On page 6, he spends two pages describing a drought, and plagues, and it's just like you would do if it were a real history book.

Interviewer: Were there other words you didn't understand?

Gabriela: I didn't understand the word *unobtrusive*, but from looking at the context clues, I'm guessing that it means that they don't get in people's way. And because it said that they avoid us, I'm guessing that's what it means.

Interviewer: That's exactly what it means.

Leisure reading immerses students in contextually rich uses of academic vocabulary within the larger contexts of effective and beautiful academic language that is acquired with minimal effort on the part of the reader. It also provides modeling for how authors use words to achieve specific purposes within their texts. If our goal is to help students independently and critically read through grade-level literature and content-area texts, then it would behoove us to start with leisure reading, where academic language is less painfully acquired. We cannot overstate the powerful effects that leisure reading has on building students' vocabulary. A critical foundation to reaching advanced levels of literacy is that we begin by immersing children in academic language within the context of great stories where they can painlessly acquire the vocabulary and sentence structures, which can facilitate their understandings of more complex readings, and even support their ownership of these words.

Cunningham and Stanovich's (2001) review of the research provides a compelling argument for the powerful effect of reading on overall vocabulary and cognitive development. When looking at student performance as it correlates to leisure reading, they provide this startling comparison: "the entire year's out-of-school reading for the child at the 10th percentile amounts to just two days reading for the child at the 90th percentile!" (p.141). What's more alarming is that the out-of-school leisure reading gap is not being bridged by in-school reading. Gambrell, Wilson, and Gantt (2001) found that during the school day, good readers spent more time actually reading, while poor readers spent more time learning about reading and practicing isolated decoding skills outside the context of meaningful stories.

There is also evidence that reading novels causes physiological changes in the brain's neural connectivity. Berns, Blaine, Prietula, and Pye (2013) set out to investigate the measurable impact that reading novels has on the brain using MRI analysis. According to the researchers, "It seems plausible that if something as simple as a book can leave the impression that one's life has been changed, then perhaps it is powerful enough to cause changes in brain function and structure." Their study found both short-term and long-term changes to the brain as a result of pre-tests, followed by a nine day reading period and follow-up tests taken five days later. Immediately following the readings, researchers found a significant increase in neural connections centered around the regions of the brain that are associated with perspective taking and story comprehension. Long-term changes in connectivity pointed to the impact that reading novels had on overall language. The researchers conclude, "Our results suggest a potential mechanism by which reading stories not only strengthen language processing regions but also affect the individual through embodied semantics in sensorimotor regions" (p. 599).

We have not addressed the power of leisure reading on overall reading development, writing ability, and grammar development. Krashen's review of the literature found that, with regard to all of these skills, leisure reading is nearly always superior to direct instruction (2004). With the rising emphases placed on the reading of informational text, it is critical that we not lose sight of the importance of the read-aloud and of building up strong foundations in leisure reading.

A Tale of Two Countries

The role of leisure reading in the United States is seeing a marked decline. While reading for 9-year-olds is at an all-time high, the older students get, the less they read. Though the amount of reading within homework and schoolwork has remained the same in the United States, "the percentage of 17-year-olds who read nothing at all for pleasure has doubled over a 20 year period." Literature reading among college graduates has also had a substantial decline, and Americans are spending less on books than at any other time in the last 20 years (National Endowment for the Arts, 2007). Most disturbing of all is that even strong readers are reading less. Some of this is influenced by the role of social media in the lives of adolescents, teens, and college graduates. McKenna et al. (2012) surveyed middle schoolers to get a feel for how reading attitudes have changed over time. They found that much of the middle schoolers' out-of-school literacies are now comprised of text produced by peers via social media. While they argue that this may create more opportunities than it does obstacles, they do emphasize that, where traditional reading is concerned, attitudes about reading have changed and gradually worsened over time.

In a *New York Times* op-ed titled "The Country That Stopped Reading," Mexican author David Toscana provides a passionate and scathing reproof to his fellow countrymen for allowing the role of literature to become less prominent among its citizens. Toscana writes, "Even if baseline literacy, the ability to read a street sign or news bulletin, is rising, the practice of reading an actual book is not. Once a reasonably well-educated country, Mexico took the penultimate spot, out of 108 countries, in a Unesco assessment of reading habits a few years ago. . . . Despite recent gains in industrial development and increasing numbers of engineering graduates, Mexico is floundering socially, politically and economically because so many of its citizens do not read."

Toscana's essay is rife with concern over the marginalization of literature in society. In describing a conversation that he had with a political leader in his home state, and emphasizing the problem with children being taught to read but not actually reading, the political leader "wondered what the point of the students' reading *Don Quixote* was. He said we needed to teach them to read the newspaper." According to Toscana, literature has become so marginalized that his daughter's literature teacher actually banned all fiction from the classroom. "We're going to read history and biology textbooks," she said, "because that way you'll read and learn at the same time."

Toscana concludes his essay with sarcastic eloquence. When referring to the educational system, he believes, "it needs to make students read, read and read. But perhaps the Mexican government is not ready for its people to be truly educated. We know that books give people ambitions, expectations, a sense of dignity. If tomorrow we were to wake up as educated as the Finnish people, the streets would be filled with indignant citizens and our frightened government would be asking itself where these people got more than a dishwasher's training." Toscana's essay may simply be one man's opinion in a country where people have had substantially different experiences with literature, and views about literature than the ones he has had, but one cannot deny that he raises important questions regarding the importance of literature in public schools.

Literacy in both informational texts and literature is important. However, we'd like to focus for a moment on the merits of literature, and on why literature ought to retain a vibrant role in our schools and in our lives. Both informational texts and literature provide opportunities for higher-order thinking, but literature does so in a very different way than informational texts do. Both are equally important. Informational texts are more compact, more dense, more technical, more focused in providing readers with solutions. Literature draws readers into alternate realities, and it can do so for extended periods of time. And, reading for extended periods of time is important, because if we don't get students to read for extended periods of time, their reading skills fail to progress (Cunningham & Stanovich, 2001). A study by the National Endowment for the Arts (2007) indicates that the older students get, the less they involve themselves with leisure reading, and there is also a striking parallel in the decline of their reading scores.

Literature and Higher-Order Thinking

Literature provides opportunities for readers to reflect on society and to critically analyze life from various perspectives. For a few hours, we see through the eyes of others. In the often quoted words of C. S. Lewis, "Literature adds to reality, it does not simply describe it. It enriches the necessary competencies that daily life requires and provides; and in this respect, it irrigates the deserts that our lives have already become." Literature allows us to add to our reality, by opening different realities that we could not practically experience without it. In describing life from different perspectives, it adds to what we know about life and prompts us to step back, compare, and reflect.

We remember reading an abridged version of *Oliver Twist* to our daughter, who was in the midst of experiencing some minor unpleasant social experiences with a few 2nd grade peers. While reading of Oliver's troubles, our daughter interrupted us and said, "His life is so hard. Are other people's lives that hard?" This led us to a discussion about life's inequities and how difficult life can be for so many people. Her social dilemmas paled in comparison. The power of a different perspective allowed her to begin exploring that reality. Great books, and subsequent discussions about great books, lead students to analyze their own reality and realities as they exist for others.

Ninth grader Alison explained that she is continuously exploring these realities as she reads. According to Alison, "Books taught me things that no one could ever teach in class. Books taught me how to relate to people. They taught me that I didn't have to be the gothic girl to understand the gothic girl; I don't have to be the popular girl to understand the popular girl; I don't have to be physically hurting to understand other's pain. Even though I haven't lived the exact life as others, I can relate to them." Alison discovered her love for reading in Keely Potter's class. It was during her 7th grade year that she found her literary first love, the book that spoke to her and that made her fall in love with reading. Potter noticed that because Alison became such an avid reader and heavily analyzed the books that she read, "her ability to think and articulate her thinking just blossomed." Ninth grader Ian also discovered his love for reading in Potter's class. When asked to describe how he had seen himself grow as a reader, he said, "I improved as a reader by using analytical skills such as inferencing, predicting, identifying theme. As for why, I'm not sure. A brilliant work can do that to you."

Kidd and Castano (2013) conducted five experiments in an effort to examine the effect of reading on specific social competencies. They compared the reading of preselected examples of literature to the reading of preselected examples of popular fiction, nonfiction, and reading nothing at all. They found that scores on tests aimed at measuring emotional intelligence and empathy were increased as a result of participants' reading of literature. In their study, the reading of literature was superior to that of reading popular fiction, nonfiction, and nothing at all in terms of measures of empathy and emotional intelligence. The study received both praise and criticism. Much of the praise came from the reliability of scores conducted over five experiments. Criticism stemmed primarily from the researcher's narrow definition of literature versus popular fiction, and the sample texts that they selected. Our own interviews with children point to evidence that both literature and popular fiction affect student perceptions of their increased empathy. To repeat what 9th grader Alison stated, books "taught me that I didn't have to be the gothic girl to understand the gothic girl." Empathy, while being a critical element to success in so many fields (for example, medicine), is not an attribute that can be easily distributed, practiced, or developed in a classroom environment. Yet there is evidence that it can be increased through the pages of a book.

Literature provides us with case studies in life. These case studies present unique opportunities to analyze characters, themes, and authors' choices. They provide opportunities to help students make connections, understand people, understand life, and question, analyze, and critically evaluate societies. Toscana is right. Reading does give people ambitions, expectations, and a sense of dignity. Reading Toscana's passionate rant, in light of the data on the declining levels of leisure reading in the Unites States, we couldn't help but wonder if, to a certain extent, we weren't also reading the words of the Ghost of Christmas Future.

Implicit and Explicit Vocabulary Development

Implicit vocabulary is developed by immersing children in comprehensible environments that are rich in academic language embedded in meaningful contexts. For example, using read-alouds is a way to foster vocabulary development implicitly. Explicitly teaching academic vocabulary involves directly teaching vocabulary. Research shows us that both implicit and explicit vocabulary teaching hold merit when they are done within a meaningful context. Because of the complexity of language and the amount of vocabulary coverage that would be necessary, a combination of both approaches toward language growth is important. Remember the history paragraph that was introduced earlier? Explicitly teaching every academic word that had been replaced with *blah* would leave little time for teaching anything else. This is especially true in light of the fact that the paragraph only makes up a small portion of what was assigned to be read. Additionally, lack of exposure to words in different contexts can often lead to misunderstandings of which students and teachers are unaware. While the one student knew that *admission* meant entry, the context in which he knew *admission* caused him to misunderstand the meaning of the sentence.

In light of what is practical, implicit vocabulary development really ought to be a critical piece of what we intentionally pursue. One of our favorite quotes regarding the complexity of language is this: "Language is too vast, too complex, to be taught or learned one rule or word at a time" (Krashen, 2004, p.18). When it comes to effectively teaching academic language, we will need to allow for students to soak in it. Helping students acquire academic language will require that we lay a thick foundation for understanding. It will take a strategic approach toward intentionally using both implicit and explicit vocabulary development.

It's also important to note that in real life and in the research, the distinction between implicit and explicit vocabulary development is not always that clear. For example, though Elley's studies included read-alouds and leisure reading, they also included interaction around the text through shared reading experiences where teachers added to students' comprehension, making the text relevant. While there was implicit language development occurring, where students *soaked* in the language, there was also explicit language development occurring, where teachers explained the meanings of words. Helping students get lost in the linguistically meaningful contexts of books will require that we do both and know when to do both. We'll review some strategies for using a healthy combination of both implicit and explicit vocabulary development within teaching contexts. We will need to be explicit in our teaching, but, because of the complexity of academic language, we'll also need to allow for students to simply experience the words.

What About English Language Learners?

According to a national survey (Educational Projects in Education, 2013), teachers showed the greatest trepidation in teaching the Common Core State Standards with English language learners (ELLs). Next in line were students with special needs. Let's focus on ELLs for a moment. On average, 12.9 percent of ELLs are exited from programs annually. At that rate, it would take eight years to exit the current pool of ELLs that entered during this school year. Consider that number paired with the fact that 65 percent of ELLs were born in the United States or its territories (Swanson, 2009). (Note: Children born in Puerto Rico are U.S.-born and included in that percentage, but they make up only 3 percent of the population of ELLs.) So, why is success in school so hard for ELLs? Why will it take about eight years to exit, or reclassify, the current pool of ELLs, especially in light of the fact that the majority were born in the United States and are likely to be conversational? The answer is simple: academic language. According to middle school English as a Second Language (ESL) teacher Georgia Jones, "The first impression that people get when I tell them that I teach ESL is that I sit in a little classroom with students, running through flashcards, 'Car,' 'Red,' 'The car is red.' No. That type of teaching is for the rare two or three students that come in midyear, and it only lasts for a few months. The majority of ELLs in my district have been in ESL for a few years already. Most of what I do is teach metacognitive skills and content reading strategies. I teach academic language. I teach kids how to ace their history class. And with most of my students, you can't even tell that they qualify for ESL because they can talk your ear off. But they can't legally exit, because they can't pass exit tests that measure academic language." In order to help ELLs succeed, especially under new, more rigorous state standards, it will take a concerted everyday effort of engaging them in text, and in interactions around text, because that is where the academic language is found.

ESL teacher Carmen Rowe explains it this way: "When you're talking about English language learners, all of the challenges that native English speakers have in becoming avid readers are magnified because they are reading in a language in which they are weaker. My job as the teacher is to help students engage in reading so that they grow to love it. And the more they love it, the more they'll do it. They need practice, practice, practice, or actual time spent reading. So every minute that they have with me is spent in books. We practice reading books, talking about books, and writing about books. I see it. Without exception, the more they read, the more linguistic and academic progress they make." Though the task of ESL teachers may seem as though it involves unfamiliar linguistically enlightened practices that focus on things like *schwas, bilabials,* and *fricatives* (we love that word), focusing on those types of things would actually make for a very poor use of a student's time. We are talking about time that ELL students simply do not have. The fact is, most of the skills that ELLs need are found within the pages of books: listening to books, reading books, talking about books, and writing about books. For students who can carry on even the most basic conversations, there are no better language models than the language found in books.

What About Students with Special Needs?

The principles in this book are for all students. While you will need to closely monitor the progress of students with unique needs, we have found that the best ways to teach students in diverse classrooms that include English language learners, students with special needs, and struggling or reluctant readers is to really engage the students in literature and informational texts. In order to succeed, it will take lots of positive interactions around text, because that is where the academic language is found. Preus (2012) found that in environments that fostered higher-order thinking and authentic learning, students with special needs performed better. Practices such as "asking open-ended questions, expecting students to provide evidence to support their answers, asking students to write down their thinking, building on student questions, modeling the thinking process, and providing specific feedback" were found to benefit all students regardless of whether or not they had disabilities (p. 76). According to Preus, "there was actually very little difference between how teachers treated students with and without disabilities. Differentiation, such as scaffolding and flexible grouping, was provided to anyone who needed it. Students without disabilities were, on average, somewhat more successful in the work than those with disabilities, but the important fact is that students with disabilities did the same work. Work was not watered down for those with disabilities" (2012, p.76).

Former special education and inclusion teacher Ashley Miller now teaches methods courses for graduate and undergraduate education majors at Millersville University. According to Miller, "When talking about students with special needs, particularly individuals with decoding, fluency, or comprehension challenges, the key for me was to provide them with extensive opportunities to build and sustain a positive relationship with literacy. In working with high school students in learning support, I first had to apprehend that reading provoked negative feelings. At some point in their lives, reading became unexciting, frustrating, and embarrassing. To combat this, I purposefully created moments where the student could see my level of respect for his reading struggle, while setting the stage for him to be successful and to academically shine in front of his peers. Some of this involved individually preparing the student for what we would be learning in class that day, so that he or she could prepare for it ahead of time. It only took me a few minutes to do this."

Miller points out the importance of the relational role of the teacher in inspiring children to take risks within a safe environment. "Throughout every lesson, regardless of the subject, all teachers have endless opportunities to have students with special needs engage in reading and build a positive experience with it. Building their self-esteem in small ways initiates the momentum necessary to open their minds and hearts to reading. With each piece of successful moments, no matter how minute, the barriers begin to fall. They begin to enjoy it and eventually are more willing to take risks and push themselves to improve."

The Answers Are in the Texts

Academic language development needs to be a priority in schools for students of all ages. This is especially true for students raised in poverty, who are least likely to be exposed to sophisticated school-like speech. In order to address this area of critical need, we need to provide students with meaningful access to where academic language is found. Academic language is most plentiful in text. This is true of well-selected literature as well as informational texts. We can help students accelerate their academic language growth by increasing the exposure that students have to academic language placed in meaningful contexts within texts. Subsequent chapters in this book will be aimed at providing you with tools for helping students gain meaningful access to deeper comprehension and analysis of what they read.

2

Tools for Developing Academic Language

Reading has had an enormous impact on my vocabulary. Every book we pick up has a new word or phrase to teach us. So every time we set a book down we walk away with words. As for me, personally, every time I find a new word or phrase in text, I immediately want to use it. I want to feel how it rolls off my tongue. Reading has given me an ever-expanding vocabulary. —Ian, 9th grade

Read, Read, and Read Some More

Earlier, we shared research findings that attest to the power of leisure reading and the read-aloud in building academic vocabulary for students. We'll sum it up briefly here. Research suggests that the very best thing that you can do to increase your students' vocabulary is to encourage leisure reading of self-selected books and participation in the read-aloud experience. Make it your goal to help your students develop a love for reading, and vocabulary will grow with minimal effort on your part. If you are not encouraging a love for reading among your students, then you are working too hard. Chances are you are trying to build reading skills and foster language development that can more easily and more authentically be taking place while students find themselves lost in a good book. Your time can be better spent on helping students explore opportunities for higher-order thinking within the book.

Additionally, when it comes to fostering a love for reading, it helps if you believe what you're selling. In other words, it helps if you yourself are a reader. If you haven't developed a love for reading yet, it's not too late. Coauthor Pérsida Himmele discovered her love for reading during her graduate studies, and she could practically feel her own vocabulary bank growing with every new book she read. She remembers finally understanding what people meant when they said that "the book was better than the movie." As a result of her new discoveries, she made it her goal to read daily to her 6th grade students. She distinctly remembers reading Michael Crichton's newly released *Jurassic Park* and looking up to see the completely captivated faces of the students in her diverse urban classroom. They were entranced—lost in a sea of big, beautiful, academic words. The power of reading is found in the fact that realities are entirely built on words alone. There are no other scaffolds, other than words— complex, abstract, hard-to-learn, academic words couched in a captivating and meaningful context.

⚙ Books That Model Academic Language (Tips and Booklist)

While it is important to provide students with a variety of read-aloud experiences and to honor students' tastes in books, it's also important to know that not all books immerse students in rich academic language experiences. When looking for books that contain high levels of academic language, choose ones that you believe will captivate students' attention and that contain examples of vocabulary and sentence structures not typically used in spoken language by children of the target age group. For example, consider the following excerpt from *The Book Thief,* by Marcus Zusak: "A boy arrived first, with cluttered breath and what appeared to be a toolbox. With great trepidation, he approached the cockpit and watched the pilot, gauging if he was alive, at which point, he still was. The book thief arrived perhaps thirty seconds later" (p. 10). Though this book is intended for students in grades 7 and up, it models vocabulary, imagery, and complex sentence structures that aren't typically used in speech by middle and high schoolers, and it does so within a rich context that will quickly engage readers and listeners. In the appendix of this book we have included a list and descriptions of books that contain rich academic language embedded within the context of wonderful stories and poetry. If you are looking for some recommendations for books that make great reads while also being packed with beautiful language, we hope that you find those listed in the appendix to be a helpful start.

⚙ Audiobooks

Chapter books in audiobook format can provide rich opportunities for exposure to academic language that can go a long way in supporting vocabulary and language growth, especially when they are sent home with struggling readers who are not yet able to read stories at their interest levels. There is growing evidence of a positive correlation between the use of audiobooks and motivation; (Beers, 1998; Bomar, 2006; Cardillo, Coville, Ditlow, Myrick, & Lesesne, 2007) increased vocabulary, writing skills, and comprehension (Patten & Craig, 2007); increased verbal fluency (Cardillo et al., 2007) and an increased use of reading strategies (Littleton, Wood, & Chera, 2006). Audiobooks can serve as a critical bridge between the listening experience and the successful reading experience. It is important to note that we are not talking about the audiobooks typically included in basal programs. These are often so poorly done that they fail to capture the imagination. We are talking about commercial audiobooks, where publishers often use accomplished actors and actresses who have seemingly no inhibitions in painting word pictures through the use of varied voices. These varied voices often serve as scaffolds for comprehension of the rich academic language in the text.

For principal Jackie Martin-Hair, a schoolwide audiobook club served to build community as well as to reinforce the value of books. Martin-Hair chose two audiobooks each year to play over the intercom in the morning while all activity in her building drew to a halt. Every faculty member, staff member, and student had a hard copy of the book to keep so they could read along while they listened to the audiobook version. According to Martin-Hair, "It has been a wonderful community-building activity, because everybody was reading it. My secretary started reading it at home with her grandchild. And, my building assistant told me, 'You got me hooked on reading again—and now I can't stop.' Any time that we can think about ourselves as readers, we're better able to communicate the importance of that to our students. I'm really pushing the metacognitive facet of reading this time around." A "Question to Go" aimed at higher-order thinking was posed by one of the students over the intercom, so that students could discuss the book after the audiobook excerpt was played. Consider using audiobooks with your students, allowing them to listen to these books as an occasional substitute for the hard copy. Audiobooks can go a long way in immersing students in academic language that is embedded within the context of a captivating story.

Focusing on Words While Reading

Selecting target vocabulary from read-alouds and focusing on the meanings of words as books are being read has been found to be an effective way of teaching vocabulary (Beck & McKeown, 2007; Biemiller, 2003; Biemiller & Boote, 2006). Biemiller and Boote's study showed average target vocabulary word gains of 12 percent with repeated readings of picture books. Adding word explanations added a gain of 10 percent for a total gain of 22 percent. According to Biemiller and Boote, "reading stories with word explanations has been shown to be more effective than simply reading stories, even when read repeatedly" (p. 46). Warwick Elley (1989) also found that explaining words while reading was more effective than not explaining words. However, as Biemiller and Boote (2006) note, in their own experiences, children don't appreciate the interruptions during first readings. Additionally, repeated readings are not an option for those teachers reading chapter books. Chopping up the flow with interruptions can really stand in the way of students getting lost in a good book. It is important to note that a 10 percent gain is still impressive (it was a 15 percent gain in Elley's 1989 study). And considering that the volume of words being read is substantially increased when reading chapter books, we'd like to make a case for reading chapter books to children as early as possible with or without explanations. When an appropriate opportunity presents itself to focus on choice words without interrupting the flow, or previewing select words, or revisiting the excerpts that contain target words, then we encourage teachers to capitalize on those opportunities.

Talk the Talk

Exposure to more sophisticated language in contexts that are comprehensible can also help in the development of students' academic language. As noted earlier, in research studies that implemented even a small adjustment of teacher or caretaker speech that embedded more sophisticated speech in adult communications with children, significant vocabulary growth took place (Hoff, 2003; Roberts & Kaiser, 2011; Ruston & Schwanenflugel, 2010; Weizman & Snow, 2001). Perhaps a more relatable example of how children learn speech through meaningful contexts is the use of slang. Children don't typically explain slang to each other—they gain the meaning from context. The same can be said about the use of academic vocabulary if we embed it in the context that is sitting before us. Using synonyms to elaborate on the words you're using can support students in their use of the words and their ability to comprehend it in print. So instead of saying something like, "Johnny, will you tell me why you wrote this?" say something like, "Johnny, will you elaborate on why you wrote this? Tell me more." Though we only briefly touched on this concept of "speaking it," or using your own speech as a verbal scaffold, we believe that the concept packs a powerful punch. What better context for learning vocabulary than the here and now?

⚙ Responding to the Moment

While teaching a unit on the civil rights movement, 8th grade social studies teacher Liz Lubeskie noticed that her students were struggling to make their way through an informational text, due to both the content and non-content-specific vocabulary words. According to Lubeskie, "there were so many words they didn't know. That's when we stopped and said, 'What words don't we know?' And we started highlighting those words. They highlighted words like *fugitive*, *abolitionist*, and *bigotry*." Lubeskie asked them to find a quote within the text, write the words they didn't know on construction paper alongside their definitions and an example of how they were used within the context of the text, and attach the pictures that represented the words. "Then, we did a gallery walk where they walked around and talked about the words." Words and concepts on the posters included terms like *fugitive slave laws*, *slave codes*, *Missouri Compromise*, *abolitionist*, *Dred Scott decision*, *Kansas Nebraska Act*, and *bigotry*. Lubeskie noted that because these words were repeatedly referenced in their text, they were able to move on with better comprehension after explicitly learning these terms.

⚙ Knowing About Words

While vocabulary is learned implicitly as well as explicitly, it is also important for students to be aware of how they can effectively manage their own vocabulary growth whenever possible. Carlo et al. (2004) found that the teaching of non-content-specific academic vocabulary had positive effects for 5th graders involved in the study. But it wasn't simply the memorization of isolated words and their meanings that seemed to make the difference. "Teaching new words was subordinated to the goal of teaching about new words—various kinds of information about words that could help children figure out word meanings on their own" (p. 205). Researchers reduced the number of words that were taught weekly and instead focused on things like teaching students how to use contexts to figure out word meanings, and how to analyze the morphological structure of the words to figure out the meanings. They concluded that "such strategies could have ongoing value to children who encounter unknown words in semantically rich contexts, who understand enough of the context to use contextual information in analyzing word meaning, and who remember to use them. Their value, at least in the short run, was in fact confirmed by our finding of a significant impact on reading comprehension" (p. 205).

⚙ Picture Word Walls

Word walls that are authentic, based on what is actually taught, and not just commercially purchased, can be an excellent way of tracking the words learned and of having something to reference, so that featured words can be used again in student writings. Eighth grade social studies teacher Liz Lubeskie's word walls are constantly changing. She uses word walls for the various history units that she teaches. The word walls contain content-specific and non-content-specific words that are important for the unit being learned at the moment. Words are discussed and put up at the point that they are being learned. The words are referenced whenever possible.

While word walls are typically used in the elementary grades, Harmon et al. (2009) studied their use in the secondary grades. They found that the best word walls were the ones that included student-created cues to help them remember the meanings. One helpful strategy was the use of interactive word walls that included a student-created picture to go alongside each word. Harmon et al. emphasize that a word wall itself doesn't teach vocabulary. By posting words authentically used, alongside student pictures, students were able to connect with the vocabulary being featured.

⚙ Picture Vocabulary Analysis

Eighth grade English teacher Matt Baker selects pictures and asks students to make connections between the pictures and the vocabulary words. "In class I might begin by showing a photograph or painting and asking students, individually or in small groups, to connect it to their vocabulary words. Their explanations of the connections are the key. I use the same method as the final assessment." The pictures selected may not immediately seem to be related to the words, but "the students are remarkably creative at matching the words to the pictures in ways that provide evidence that they have grasped the meaning of the words." When asked whether or not he spends a great deal of time finding pictures, he responded, "It is very easy to find pictures on the Internet. I use *National Geographic* quite a bit. The activity creates a nice challenge for the students."

It takes really analyzing a word's meaning to be able to find its meaning within a picture. That analysis goes beyond just comprehending the meaning of a word, but requires that students look at the word from different angles and connect the words to a picture that may not seemingly match the literal definition of the word. Baker will also ask students to tear out pictures from magazines and ask them, "How many words can you find that fit that picture?" Baker has found that this method is more effective than more traditional vocabulary teaching methods that he has used in the past. "With the traditional 'match up the definitions' type of activities, they were never able to remember the meanings, but when I started doing it this way, I found that the students would start using those words when they were writing or when they were explaining things to me." This may very well be due to the processing that it took in order to analyze the word and find ways to see it portrayed in a picture that isn't seemingly related.

⚙ Collecting and Celebrating Words

Keely Potter repeatedly uses the phrases *collecting words* and *celebrating words* with her 5th through 8th grade students. According to Potter, "I put so much emphasis on the students writing about the words. And I will point it out when they do this. As long as they give credit to where they got it from, they can say 'inspired by.' I tell them, 'Words are what we borrow.'" Potter also encourages her students to make use of the language arts content vocabulary from their reading response tool sheets (see Chapter 4, Figures 4.5, 4.6, and 4.7). "I regularly highlight words in their reading responses that are from the tool sheet. If they say, 'The perspective for this story was written in first person,' then I'll highlight the words 'perspective' and 'first person.' I'll celebrate the fact that they're using content vocabulary, and they are making it relevant." This celebration of words was evident in Potter's students' responses to interviews and reflection questions. Seventh grader Hayley responded, "I track the details and word choice, the ideas, whether it's first or third person, and connections. We put all of that together and make good fresh sentences." According to Potter, "I think the big thing with the academic vocabulary is that we, as teachers, understand how powerful words can be. It is so important that we celebrate words."

In order to help students pause and reflect on new words, Figure 2.1 provides a place for students to analyze these in the form of bookmarks. These

Figure 2.1

Celebrating Words Bookmark and Collecting Words Bookmark

CELEBRATING WORDS	COLLECTING WORDS
As you read, identify words that the author uses to set a tone or mood in this book. Write down the words and the page numbers, and brief notes to help you remember why you picked those words.	As you read, identify new words that you've collected. Write down the words and the page numbers, and brief notes to help you remember what you think the word means. Try to confirm these later, by asking the teacher, using the Internet, or using a dictionary.

bookmarks allow readers to record these words without heavily disrupting their reading flow. Potter encourages students to collect words throughout their reading. She describes the progress she's seen in the reading and vocabulary of one 7th grader, in particular, and one experience with a word he collected. "Tanner has become an avid reader in my room. One day last year in class he said, 'I have an epiphany.' So now, Tanner is the keeper of the word *epiphany*. Whenever we come across that word, students will say, 'That's Tanner's word.'" Figure 2.1 includes bookmarks that can foster the habit of identifying interesting words and noticing how the author uses the new words. They also provide a scaffold for conversation if you are holding reading conferences and want to discuss word choice. The bookmarks can be kept separate, photocopied back to back, or copied together and folded so that students focus on both aspects of word choice.

Savoring Words Prompts

High school English teachers Susan Grammer and Shaun Karli developed a series of questions that help students to pause and savor the words they come across in their texts. They also encourage students to analyze the author's usage of these words. Their template of questions (Figure 2.2) has been used with a variety of teacher-selected excerpts on which they ask students to focus.

Figure 2.2
Savoring Words

Step 1: Circle the words that stand out to you.

Step 2: Study those words to determine why they stand out. Consider ALL of the following possibilities:

- Do the words stand out because they are unexpected? In what way are they unexpected?
- Do the words stand out because of the sounds they create? If so, what are the sounds?
- Do the words stand out because of the image they conjure? If so, what is the image?
- Do the words stand out because of the rhythm they provide? If so, what kind of rhythm?
- Do the words stand out because of a strong connotation they are associated with? If so, what connotation?

Step 3: If different words were used, what would be lost? (Try substituting words for the circled words.)

Step 4: Since these words are used, what idea is suggested or reinforced?

Step 5: What type of figurative language did the author use?

Step 6: Is the figurative language effective? Why? Why not?

Developed by Susan Grammer and Shaun Karli. Used with permission.

⚙ Academic Versus Spoken Language

As educators, we know that there is a difference between conversational language and academic language. There are quantifiable and complicated aspects to academic language that make it different from spoken language. Although educators might be aware of these differences, most students are only vaguely aware of what makes informational texts difficult. When 7th grader Ridge was asked to explain why he didn't like informational texts, he answered, "Nonfiction has harder words." That is certainly a start, because he's thinking about it and he has noticed that the vocabulary usage in nonfiction is different. But taking a brief detour in explaining what makes informational texts difficult could be a step in helping students actively attempt to figure it out. This could not be more true than with those for whom academic language is most difficult. ESL teacher Yara Graupera-Richardson took an explicit approach to teaching about language after she realized that her students were attributing their challenges to innate intellectual weaknesses. After teaching about the basic differences between conversational and academic language, and the fact that it takes years to master academic language, she started noticing that her students would reassure each other regarding the process of making it through tasks that required academic language. Rather than internalize their lack of success as evidence of their innate weaknesses or inability to complete the task, they began talking about what it would take to successfully complete the task, given that it required the use of academic language. According to Graupera-Richardson, "I think that's the best thing I did this year, and it was so simple."

Metacognition essentially refers to the act of thinking about thinking. When students are able to self-regulate learning by thinking about their own thinking, they perform better (Goos, Galbraith, & Renshaw, 2002; Kramirski & Mevarech, 2003; Kuhn, 2000). That process is enhanced when they develop metacognitive skills together in cooperative learning settings as compared to developing these skills individually (Kramirski & Mevarech, 2003). To facilitate the development of metacognitive skills, we encourage teachers to consider explicitly presenting these challenges to students, and then helping students individually and collectively brainstorm solutions that would allow them to take ownership of the process of improving proficiency in reading informational texts. Our philosophy is simple: It's easier to climb a mountain if you know ahead of time the types of challenges you may encounter. And it's especially easier if you know that each of the challenges is, in fact, surmountable with the right tools, the right mindset, and the right strategies.

Presenting the truth regarding the challenges to students also takes a safe environment where risk taking is welcomed. It takes the right amounts of truth and encouragement. On the one hand, students need to know that the task is challenging. On the other hand, they need to know that they are capable of tackling the challenge. ESL teacher Carmen Rowe is often responsible for teaching language arts to students whose reading levels are woefully behind that of their peers. According to Rowe, "I never sugarcoated it. And I had to support them through their angst. But I had to be completely and totally honest about the challenges that they were facing. I laid out the books that they were able to read, right next to the pile that were assigned to students reading closer to grade level. And I told them, 'Right now, you can read these types of books, but the more we practice, the better you'll get. And my goal is that you'll be able to read these kinds of books.' They knew that I believed they could do it, so they practiced, practiced, practiced. They moved up several grade levels in one year. And when they saw themselves grow, they were so proud. We celebrated every success. But I couldn't have done that unless I had been upfront with them, so that they knew that they'd need to put in twice the effort as the other students. And they did."

Whether you teach ELLs or those for whom English is their only language, the language in informational texts is complicated. Students need to know that struggling with the language in informational texts is not due to their innate weaknesses or lack of ability. The language is challenging for everybody. But, with the right strategies, they can tackle these challenges. Nagy and Townsend (2012) review the research on what makes academic language so difficult when compared to spoken language. Their review lays out six components of academic language that make it challenging for students:

1. Latin and Greek vocabulary

2. Morphologically complex words

3. More nouns, adjectives, and prepositions

4. Grammatical metaphor, including nominalizations

5. Informational density

6. Abstractness

Figure 2.3 provides a student-friendly overview of Nagy and Townsend's six components of academic language, using examples and terms that children would more easily comprehend. Note that to facilitate student comprehension,

Figure 2.3

Student-Friendly Comparison of Academic and Spoken Language

Why Is This So Hard?
Academic Language vs. The Language We Speak

1. **Academic words have different origins.**
   Academic vocabulary often has Latin and Greek origins. Spoken words usually have Germanic origins. Words with Germanic origins are words we use every day, so we're used to them and they're easier to understand.

2. **Academic words are longer.**
   Academic words often have more than one prefix and suffix. For example the word *denationalization* comes from the root word *nation.* The word went from *nation*, to *national*, to *nationalize*, to *nationalization*, to *denationalization*. All of those small parts of meaning (affixes) make the word long and hard to figure out. In case you're wondering, *denationalization* refers to the removal of national rights or characteristics. (In academic terms, this feature of academic language is referred to as morphological complexity.)

3. **Academic language uses more nouns, adjectives, and prepositions.**
   Written academic language contains more nouns, adjectives, and prepositions than spoken language, making it less familiar and more complex.

4. **Academic language uses everyday words in new and unfamiliar ways.**
   One of the trickiest things about academic language is the way it makes use of everyday words and gives them completely different meanings, or uses them in ways that the words aren't typically used. For example, when talking about President Ulysses S. Grant, the author of a 5th grade text states, "He had disliked the fancy trappings of high military rank"(Viola, 1998, p. 646). The word *fancy* is well-known, and the word *trapping* ought to be a form of a verb, but together they create a new word that functions as a noun: *the fancy trappings*. But if you're still looking at the two individual words, *fancy* and *trappings,* it can be very confusing. In the text, *fancy trappings* is referring to things that trap people's attentions. (In academics terms, this feature of academic language is referred to as "grammatical metaphor" and "nominalizations.")

5. **Academic language packs quite a bit of information into every sentence.**
   Academic language has more ideas crammed into fewer words. When you read these kinds of sentences, you'll find that you often have to go back and reread them, just to make sense of them. For example compare the length of the two sentences you just read with this italicized sentence, which contains the same ideas but uses academic language: *With academic language, the density of information within the context of fewer words requires more careful scrutiny on the part of the reader.* Researchers have counted and found that academic language contains more ideas in fewer words and more words in fewer clauses. (In academic terms, this feature of academic language is referred to as "informational density.")

6. **Academic language uses abstract, hard-to-describe words.**
   The words used in informational texts can be pretty abstract. They are often hard to describe. It's harder to describe words like *vague* and *random* than it is to describe, or even to draw, words like *smile* or *apple*.

7. **Academic language uses technical terms.**
   Some of the words you come across will only ever apply to that specific topic you're reading about. The words tend to be unfamiliar, and you may never see them in any other contexts.

Become an expert at understanding what you read! One of the reasons that you'll need to get good at reading academic language is that it is the type of language that adults use to communicate formal messages. Imagine getting a letter explaining that you're being sued or that you will be fined if you don't do something specific. It will be written in academic language, and you'll need to be able to understand it.

Start developing and recording your comprehension strategies when reading academic texts. The next time you notice any of these features in informational texts, jot them down. See if you can come up with strategies for determining meanings. Record the strategies that worked for you so that you can share them with your teachers and your peers, and so that you can become an expert at understanding and using academic language.

By Pérsida and William Himmele, based on William Nagy and Dianna Townsend, 2012.

we divided the sixth component into two. The final paragraph in Figure 2.3 is important. Rather than leaving students with a feeling of hopelessness, it asks students to keep track of academic language and to share what worked for them. The overview is useful only as a reference. It would not be effective or beneficial to have students held accountable for learning these components. We do encourage teachers to follow up on students' metacognitive abilities to monitor their own learning, as they keep track of what is working, as well as to follow up on students' abilities to notice how authors truncate their thoughts to create formal academic-sounding passages.

⚙ Academic Language Display

As a class, it may be interesting to make note of some of the more infrequently used characteristics that appear in Figure 2.4 when students are reading informational texts. An Academic Language Display that is dedicated to this concept, and that allows students to add to it, can focus on showcasing how authors of informational texts actually used these complex concepts. When the students individually notice these, or when the topic comes up while the text is being referenced in a whole-class setting, these examples can be quickly added to the Academic Language Display.

Ask students to pay close attention to when the author makes use of any of the following techniques:

Morphological complexities: Words with multiple prefixes or suffixes
Grammatical metaphor: Common words that take on new meanings
Nominalizations: New nouns formed by combining verbs, adjectives, or other parts of speech
Information density: Shorter sentences that are packed with ideas

Make a big deal of celebrating the analytical and metacognitive skills that it took in order to notice these attributes in the author's use of words. Note: We did not reference some of the more common elements of academic language (abstract and technical vocabulary), because these appear so frequently in informational text that the display may end up being more distracting than it is helpful.

Conclusion

Many of the tools and strategies included in this chapter allow for an increased awareness and analysis of words: how they work, why they work, and how authors use words to convey and enhance a message. The goals of these strategies go beyond merely comprehending words, but allow for students to pause and savor words and the potential power that they hold in effectively communicating thoughts. The next three chapters focus on developing deep thinkers as students make sense of literature and informational texts.

3

Tools for Students' Uses of Higher-Order Thinking While Reading

For example, [the teacher] might ask, "Who influenced you the most, and why?" If she had asked me that in 6th grade, I would have sat there for 20 minutes before I could begin to answer it. Now I automatically know how to answer that. She has this chart in the back of the room with 6 levels, and she has questions on there, and you have to be on a high level of thinking on that chart. —Alexis, 8th grade

It wasn't until several years into our teaching that we started to really understand the importance of higher-order thinking. Although we had used list after list of verbs that corresponded to the six levels of Bloom's taxonomy in attempting to write higher-order objectives (and, to be honest, these were mostly done in preparation for formal observations), deep understanding didn't come to us until later. It took having enough experiences with students to know that parroting back content, performing well on tests, and forgetting everything that was supposedly learned was never going to prepare our students for making a difference in the world. As long as students were only giving us a weakened version of what we had *covered* in class, content was never going to be truly retained or made relevant to them. Furthermore, the lists of verbs often associated with Bloom's taxonomy were misleading. For example, verbs like *identify* and *create*, though typically assigned to the levels Knowledge and Synthesis, could accurately be attributed to several of Bloom's levels. A student might be asked to identify the top three critical areas of conflict that led to a major historical event. Though the verb *identify* is typically assigned to the lowest level of understanding, if the three critical areas have not been spelled out for the student, this task of identifying them might require careful analysis. The verb *create*, on the other hand, has been typically associated with higher-order thinking. But a student could create a list of six legislators without expending much cognitive muscle at all, assuming they are just rattling off what was told to them.

Part of our growth toward a deeper understanding of higher-order thinking was a result of experience and maturity, but we attribute much of our blossoming in understanding to wonderful mentors who poured into our lives a deep appreciation for inquiry. One mentor in particular, Dan Doorn at Azusa Pacific University, was living on a different wavelength entirely. Rather than provide quick answers, he consistently probed and asked questions. These questions helped us to think about what really mattered in teaching and learning, and the questions profoundly affected our teaching. Higher-order thinking begins with questions. What really matters? Ultimately, that's what we ought to be asking, and we ought to be asking that right alongside our students. Ninth grader Ian experienced a similar awakening to inquiry as a student in Keely Potter's class. According to Ian, "I've always questioned the words of a book, but Ms. Keely gave me better questions to ask, such as questioning word choice, the author's voice, and how the plot's events delivered a theme. With questioning you then go broader into making connections, seeing how the book relates to other texts, how it relates to world events, and most importantly, how it related to you on a personal level."

This chapter is about higher-order thinking. However, we are taking a very different approach than the approaches we have taken in past writings. This time, influenced by Potter, we focus on higher-order thinking with a student-powered component. Potter's own development in her understanding of higher-order thinking was a result of learning about it with her students. In her own words, "It feels like I've gotten 50 flip charts on Bloom's taxonomy during my career. But the problem that I see is that those are teacher-driven. I think that one of the most powerful ways to develop higher-order thinking is to begin to learn about it in class, alongside the students. That's why I posted Bloom's levels of thinking on my wall. I don't hide anything from them."

This chapter provides teachers with tools to help them focus on higher-order thinking right alongside their students. We include a student-friendly chart on higher-order thinking (Figure 3.1) that aims to foster the transfer of understandings on higher-order thinking to students. We also include two lists of analytical questions (Figures 3.2 and 3.3) that can be used in varieties of ways. The chart and lists can be photocopied onto colored paper, laminated, or enlarged onto posters so that they can be posted on classroom walls. In other words, as teachers are developing their own deeper understandings of higher-order thinking, their students will also be developing their understandings of higher-order thinking.

Having the display on the wall allows teachers to reference it while teaching. While modeling thinking, a teacher might say something like "All right, my brain needs to pause right now, because I'm really looking into the minds of these characters. I can retell what is happening, but that is really only lower-order thinking. To jump to higher-order thinking I'll want to start analyzing what the character's motives might be." Potter has found that students mimic her use of the higher-order thinking chart and are even able to identify the differences between higher-order thinking and lower-order thinking. When 8th grader Alexis was asked to tell about how she was able to improve her reading responses, she responded by referencing the levels of thinking. According to Alexis, "I would start to retell, but before I did that I would pull myself back. Before I retold the theme, I would explain why I thought it was a theme, or why I thought this was an important part. I didn't want to label it too much, 'the rise in action is this, and the fall in action was that.' Instead, I labeled it just a little bit, and I did it in a way that was a high-level thinking."

Focusing on higher-order thinking is powerful. It does more than simply teach content. It has the power to change students' abilities to think about the content as it relates to their world. Miri, David, and Uri (2007) found that when teachers used strategies that embedded real-world problems and open-ended class discussions that fostered inquiry-based learning, students showed an increase in their critical thinking as measured by truth seeking, open-mindedness, self-confidence in their own critical thinking, and an ability to make better decisions. In Preus's study (2012), lessons that focused on the development of higher-order thinking were characterized by instruction that included "asking open-ended questions, expecting students to provide evidence to support their answers, asking students to write down their thinking, building on student questions, modeling the thinking process and providing specific feedback." Most interesting of all was that the culture of respect encouraged a climate of fostering higher-order thinking, and that higher-order thinking, in turn, fostered a climate of respect. Zohar (2003) and Preus (2012) found that the benefits of instruction that focused on the development of higher-order thinking were experienced by both high- and low-achieving students alike.

A Brief Look at Higher-Order Thinking and Two Common Critiques

Some debate has been stirred about whether the order of the levels in Bloom's taxonomy (Bloom, 1956) actually represents the sequential order of how people learn skills and whether the taxonomy could be boiled down to a more accurate picture of cognitive processes as opposed to a level of knowledge learned. Noteworthy revisions of Bloom's taxonomy and other deeper taxonomies include work by researchers such as Anderson and Krathwohl (2001), Marzano, Pickering, and McTighe (1993), and Marzano and Kendall (2007). Each expand on the work of Bloom. We acknowledge that thoroughly understanding differences in cognitive engagement and the processes involved is a very worthy science. However, because of widespread familiarity with it, we've chosen to stick to the use of Bloom's original taxonomy in this text.

For the record, we do not ascribe to the view that people learn skills in this hierarchal sequence. Learning is much more complex and much more interconnected than any model could show. With regard to the debate over whether some of the skills should be reversed, particularly in the case of synthesis and evaluation, we feel that the level of cognitive complexities used in both are highly dependent on the task and on students' prior experiences with the tasks. In our view, the most important distinctions that can be made are those between lower-order thinking and higher-order thinking. Here is the most important difference between lower-order thinking and higher-order thinking: When it comes to lower-order thinking, students give you nothing new. They give you back what you gave them or what the book gave them. The material learned goes through no changes. It pretty much looks the same. For example, even in the case of application, where students are applying a learned skill, subtraction, to a new problem that includes new numbers, the students have done little to insert their own understandings or their own manipulation of learned material to the problem at hand. However, with higher-order thinking, the students are asked not to return what was given to them, by way of teacher delivery or another method, but to take what was given to them and manipulate the material in some way. The answers aren't in the book, though they can use the book to arrive at the answers. Higher-order thinking requires that students carefully examine certain components (analysis), take concepts learned and combine them to create something unique (synthesis), or evaluate something using the concepts that they learned as the criteria by which the worthiness of their evaluation will be judged (evaluation). Higher-order thinking is where we give students the tools that they will need in order to meaningfully interact with the content in ways that will allow them to remember it, because they took an active role in building their own deep understandings of the content and how it affects the world around them.

Knowledge

Bloom refers to the most basic level of knowing as "knowledge." Knowledge is referred to as "Remembering Facts" in Figure 3.1. This level of thinking involves basic recall and remembering. Bloom best illustrates this level, and the limited mileage it gives us, when he shares this story about John Dewey. "Almost everyone has had the experience of being unable to answer a question involving recall when the question is stated in one form, and then having little difficulty in remembering the necessary information when the question is restated in another form. This is well illustrated by John Dewey's story in which he asked a class, 'What would you find if you dug a hole in the earth?' Getting no response, he repeated the question; again he obtained nothing but silence. The teacher chided Dr. Dewey. 'You're asking the wrong question.' Turning to the class, she asked, 'What is the state of the center of the earth?' The class replied in unison, 'Igneous fusion'" (Bloom, 1956, p. 29). Knowledge refers to the shallowest level of cognitive intensity that requires little more than remembering or recall.

Where reading is concerned, a task requiring knowledge might look something like this:
Teacher: What color was the truck in the story?
Student: The truck was orange.

Using a geometry example, a task requiring knowledge might look something like this:
Teacher: What shape is this?
Student: It's a square.

Figure 3.1

Student-Friendly Higher-Order Thinking Chart

Aiming for Higher-Order Thinking

Lower-Order Thinking only uses information that has been taught to you. It does not require that you use anything other than what was already given to you in the readings or in other ways by your teacher.

1. **Remembering Facts:** Requires **basic identifying, recalling, or naming.**
   Teacher: Who is the main character?
   Student: His name is James.

2. **Retelling:** Requires **basic retelling of surface understanding without needing to deeply understand.**
   Teacher: What is the story about?
   Student: It starts off with…

3. **Applying:** Requires **basic showing in the way it was taught to you.**
   Teacher: Read this for me. I want to test your application of reading skills as measured by your fluency. (Fluency measures things like how quickly and accurately you read.)
   Student: (The student reads the text, while the teacher checks for fluency.)

Higher-Order Thinking uses information that was *not directly taught to you.* The key with higher-order thinking is that you're not just repeating what the teacher told you. With higher-order thinking you are inserting a little bit of your own brainpower into the mix.

4. **Analyzing:** Requires **deeper investigations, and looking at things from various angles.**
   Teacher: Tell me about the themes that you see developing?
   Student: I notice the themes of fear and friendship. The theme of fear is developed when . . . .

5. **Combining and Creating:** Requires **you to take what you've learned and combine it to create something that you weren't taught or shown how to do.**
   Teacher: Now that we've read and analyzed three different Roald Dahl books, I'd like you to create a description of the author's writing style that takes into account the elements that are unique to Roald Dahl's writings.
   Student: (The student creates a description of the author's writing style that takes into account the elements, from all three books, that are distinct to Roald Dahl.)

6. **Evaluating:** Requires **you to make judgments that are *based* on what you've learned.**
   Teacher: I'm going to read you a rather negative review of Roald Dahl's writings. I want you to evaluate it based on what you know about his writing style and the content of the books that we've read. Prepare an argument either supporting what was written in the review, or refuting (arguing against) what was written in the review. Be sure to include evidence from what you have read.
   Student: (The student writes the response to the review including evidence from what was read.)

By Pérsida and William Himmele, based on Bloom's taxonomy (Bloom, 1956)

Comprehension

According to Bloom (1956), comprehension "represents the lowest level of understanding (it is referred to as "Retelling" in Figure 3.1). It refers to a type of understanding or comprehension such that the individual knows what is being communicated and can make use of the material or idea being communicated without necessarily relating it to other material or seeing its fullest implications"(p. 204). It refers to a literal understanding of what was taught.

Where reading is concerned, a task requiring comprehension might look something like this:

Teacher: I would like you to summarize Chapter 3.
Student: (The student summarizes the chapter.)

Using our geometry example, a task requiring comprehension might look something like this:

Teacher: What do you remember learning yesterday about squares?
Student: Squares have four equal sides.

Application

Application refers to the use of abstractions in particular situations (it is referred to as "Applying" in Figure 3.1). We often see application used in mathematics. Students learn an abstract formula and apply it using new numbers. The skill of application in reading is typically used when students are asked to apply their reading skills.

Where reading is concerned, a task requiring application might look something like this:

Teacher: I would like you to sound out this word for me.
Student: (The student sounds out the word.)

Using our geometry example, a task requiring application might look something like this:

Teacher: Draw a square.
Student: (The student draws a square.)

Analysis

Analysis is referred to as "Analyzing" in Figure 3.1. When referring to analysis, we often use the imagery of a zoom lens. To analyze you might zoom in to get a really good look at how the different parts work together and how they affect one another. Or, you might zoom out to see how the concepts are affected by the things around them. Bloom (1956) describes analysis as "the breakdown of communication into its constituent elements or parts such that the relative hierarchy of ideas is made clear and/or the relations between the ideas expressed are made explicit" (p. 205). In reading, we use analysis when we do things like look for evidence of the author's purpose within a text.

Where reading is concerned, a task requiring analysis might look something like this:

Teacher: What symbolism do you notice with the author's use of that term? And, how does it relate to the themes that are being developed?
Student: The use of the term is symbolic of . . . . I believe that the author is using it to develop the themes of fairness and . . . .

Using our geometry example, a task requiring analysis might look something like this:

Teacher: What other things do you notice about this square?
Student: I notice that it is also a parallelogram.

Synthesis

Synthesis requires that students gather up all that they have learned and put these learned concepts together to create something that is unique (it is referred to as "Combining and Creating" in Figure 3.1). Bloom (1956) describes synthesis as "the putting together of elements and parts so as to form a whole. This involves the process of working with pieces, parts, elements, etc., and arranging and combining them in such a way as to constitute a pattern or structure not clearly there before" (p. 206). Within reading tasks, a teacher might ask students to review several works by the same author and create a profile of the author's writing style.

Where reading is concerned, a task requiring synthesis might look something like this:

Teacher: I would like you to artistically represent the various themes that are being presented in this text, and express how the author develops these themes and how the themes impact how the book functions overall.

Student: (Creates a display that artistically presents the author's use of elements such as themes, symbolism, and character development, and shows how these allow the book to function as it does.)

Using our geometry example, a task requiring synthesis might look something like this:

Teacher: I'd like you to combine everything you know about squares and parallelograms to create part of a study resource that can help you and your friends as you examine the unique attributes of various parallelograms.

Student: (Students take what they have learned about squares and parallelograms, and attempt to create an exhaustive list of each of the parallelogram's characteristics, where each parallelogram is described in a way that rules out the other parallelograms.)

Evaluation

Evaluation refers to evidence-based judgments and defenses (it is referred to as "Evaluating" in Figure 3.1). It is not simply giving an opinion. The opinion must be based on the content that was learned. As noted earlier, it requires that learners evaluate something using the concepts that they learned as the criteria by which the worthiness of their evaluation will be judged. According to Bloom (1956), evaluation refers to "judgments about the value of material and methods for given purposes . . . judgments about the extent to which material and methods satisfy criteria" (p. 207). In reading, evaluation tasks might require learners to make evidence-based judgments about the contents of the book.

Where reading is concerned, a task requiring evaluation might look something like this:

Teacher: This book has been described as a book that exposes the innate weaknesses of man and portrays man as being ultimately evil. Do you agree or disagree? Be prepared to explain why, using evidence from the text.

Student: (Students prepare an argument supporting, or refuting, the prompt using evidence from the text to support their claims.)

Using our geometry example, a task requiring evaluation might look something like this:

Teacher: Let's look at all of the study resources that we have and make sure that they are accurate, based on what we know about parallelograms.

Student: Based on what I know about parallelograms, I can tell you that your definition of a square is incomplete. All squares also need to have 90-degree angles.

⚙ Student-Friendly Higher-Order Thinking Chart

When it comes to having the levels posted, Potter says, "I am constantly going to the chart and pointing things out like, 'This is Level 2 thinking, retell. You should be at Level 4 thinking. What should that look like? What should that sound like?' This has really helped the students self-monitor where they are in their minds. It also assists with peer editing. That is the core, the skeleton. It's what we all strive for, that chart, and we all refer to it." There are benefits to having the levels posted, rather than passing out charts. On the one hand, it is a reminder for teachers to strive for higher-order thinking development. On the other hand, it's more accessible to students. According to Potter, "I've gone through different attempts to give the students a copy, to keep a copy of it, but nothing works as well as just having it on the wall. They don't have to hold it in their hands. They don't have to look for it." The posted chart serves as one type of a scaffold for 6th grader Phillip, who said, "The levels of questions inspire you to think, talk, and write." If you don't have access to convenient poster makers, a simple alternative is to copy the chart onto colored paper, or laminate copies so that students can easily find them and reference them. Figure 3.1 is a chart based on Bloom's taxonomy that is presented in student-friendly terms rather than the traditional terms. In order to help students understand the terms, we use hypothetical scenarios involving Roald Dahl's book *James and the Giant Peach.*

⚙ Prompts for Analyzing Texts

Asking the right questions can go a long way in helping students analyze texts. Figures 3.2 and 3.3 provide an assortment of analytical questions for

Figure 3.2

Prompts for Analyzing Literature

Analyzing Literature

Remember: Don't just retell—*examine closely, explain why,* and *cite evidence!*

Exploring Interconnectedness

1. Discuss some of the Elements of Fiction and how they impact the text or each other (setting, characters, plot, exposition, rising action, climax, falling action, resolution, themes, style, symbolism).

2. What are the various story lines, and how do they affect each other?

3. What is dispensable in this story? What pieces could have been removed without altering the main story? If you had to eliminate a chapter, with minimal harm to the book, which would it be? Why?

4. What is indispensable in this story? What pieces were essential to making the story work as it does?

5. In what ways might you artistically represent the Elements of Fiction within this story?

6. Suppose you were to create a movie about this text. Describe the kind of music or soundtrack that you would use for the various parts. Explain why.

Exploring Characterization

7. Which are the most and least interesting characters? Why?

8. What makes the characters believable or not believable?

9. Whom might the characters represent in real life? Draw connections between the characters and certain personality types in society or in your world.

Exploring Themes and Ideas

10. What themes do you see developing?

11. How does the author use symbolism to develop the story?

12. How does the author use metaphors to develop the story?

13. How does the book present us with metaphors of life?

14. How are everyday issues reflected in this book?

15. What are some of the important life questions that this text raises?

16. What principles might be learned from this text?

17. If you were to draw connections between this book and concepts that you have learned in social studies or science, what would those connections be?

18. What questions were left unanswered?

19. If the author were to write a follow-up text that continued along this theme, what do you believe should be included?

Exploring Author's Voice

20. What specific words does the author use to make a case for, and against, certain characters?

21. How does the author drop in subtle or not-so-subtle descriptions or events to make you like or dislike a character?

22. How does the author set the moods for this story?

23. How did the author use words to create settings that made you feel certain ways (safe/unsafe, comfortable/uncomfortable)?

24. Make some inferences with regard to what the author's ideal world would look like? What causes you to make those inferences?

Exploring Author's Voice (*continued*)

25. Refer to the more vivid images in your mind. How did the author use language to create the more vivid images in your mind?

26. If you were to read this book out loud, what emotions would you give to certain parts? What voices would you use in certain parts? Why?

27. What do you know about the author(s)? How does the author live within the text?

28. To what other authors would you compare this author? Why?

29. How would you characterize this author's style that makes it different than that of other authors?

30. Select an excerpt, or piece of text, that you felt was the most interesting or the best worded. What made it the most interesting or the best worded?

By Pérsida and William Himmele.

Figure 3.3
Prompts for Analyzing Informational Texts

Analyzing Informational Texts
Remember: Don't just retell—*examine closely, explain why,* and *cite evidence!*
Exploring Ideas

1. What are the issues being raised?

2. What questions were left unanswered?

3. Why do you believe that this was an important enough concept to include in your curriculum this year? Is its inclusion appropriate? Why/Why not?

4. What are the bigger messages being conveyed in this text?

5. What were some of the important life questions that this text raises?

6. What principles might be learned from this text?

7. If the author were to write a follow-up text that continued along this theme, what do you believe should be included?

8. Suppose you were to create a documentary about the concepts in this text. Describe the kind of music or soundtrack that you would use for the various parts. Tell why.

9. The really important thing about this set of concepts is . . .

Exploring Interconnectedness

10. How does this issue lead to other issues in life?

11. What aspects of everyday life are affected by the concepts in this text?

12. For whom are these concepts most important? Why?

13. Who might dislike or disagree with what is presented in this text? Why?

14. Whom do the concepts in this text benefit? How might they benefit from this text becoming widely publicized?

15. Whom do the concepts in this text not benefit? How might they be harmed from this text becoming widely publicized?

16. Brainstorm all the people or things that are affected by the information contained in this text. Tell how they are affected.

(continued)

Figure 3.3

Prompts for Analyzing Informational Texts

17. Say you were to become an expert in these types of concepts. How might they enhance your life?
18. What occupations would be open to experts in this knowledge?
19. How has history been affected by the type of information contained in this text?
20. How have people's personal histories been affected by the type of information contained in this text?
21. How are the contents of this text a reflection of the times in which it was written? How does it represent a snapshot of society during a specific timeframe?
22. In a hundred years, how do you think this issue might be presented?

Exploring Author's Approach, Voice, or Bias

23. What was the author's purpose in writing this text? What other purposes are there?
24. How did the author achieve his/her purpose(s)?
25. Discuss parts that were creatively worded in order to achieve a specific purpose.
26. What do you know about the author(s)? What is the author's bias? How does the author live within the text?
27. How would you characterize this author's style that makes it different from that of other authors?
28. How did the author set tones, convince, create a sense of urgency, or create moods that enhanced the message of this text?
29. Make some inferences with regard to what the author's ideal world would look like. What causes you to make those inferences?
30. If you were to read this text out loud, what tone would be used? How does the author "sound" to you? What words or stylistic traits make you think that?

By Pérsida and William Himmele.

helping students analyze literature and informational texts. The questions for analyzing literature explore concepts unique to literature, such as the Elements of Fiction, while the questions for analyzing informational texts explore things like issues being raised, relevance, and author's bias. In some instances, the same or similar questions can be asked of both literature and informational text. The questions can be used in several ways:

- They can be a resource for teachers to help students delve deeply into certain aspects of the text. If teachers use them as a resource, then they'd simply select one or more questions and fit them into their instruction.
- They can be used as a resource for students. If they are enlarged and posted somewhere in the room, teachers can simply tell students, "I'd like you to answer number 3 in your notebooks." Or, the lists can be copied onto colored paper or laminated to make them more

easily recognizable, and used as a year-long resource in student folders. For particular assignments, teachers can identify which questions should be embedded within certain reading responses or which questions ought to receive special attention while reading.

- They can be used during interactive activities. For example, in Chapter 6, we discuss an activity called Bell Networking, where students stand up and talk to someone with whom they haven't spoken that day and respond to a teacher-selected prompt. At the sound of a bell, students then find another person to discuss the next teacher-selected prompt. That continues until several prompts are discussed. The prompts can be pulled straight from these lists.

Eighth grade teacher Liz Lubeskie has predetermined question starters that she will occasionally send home with the students. She gives each of the students a different question starter, so that when they come back to class, they have all looked at the same issues from different perspectives and are now ready to talk about them. Lubeskie asks students to add dates to the questions they respond to, so that they are not always answering the same type of question. In the same way, different questions can be distributed to each of the students, so that they are responding to the same text from a different angle and are able to share these with their peers.

How the Author Lives in the Text

In addition to higher-order thinking opportunities that are found within texts, there are also wonderful opportunities when it comes to exploring aspects about the text. For example, how is the author's personal perspective, or bias, evidenced in the text? How does the author live within the pages of the text? While this question is not always easily explored for lesser-known writers, it is often easy enough to find for authors who have made a name for themselves, for whom short biographical sketches are included within works, or for whom personal interviews have been made accessible via the Internet. For example, in the book *James and the Giant Peach*, the main character, James, finds himself plucked from a happy loving home into the homes of two miserable and hateful aunts. In the story, 4-year-old James loses both of his parents to a dreadful accident. Dahl writes, "Now this, as you can well imagine, was a rather nasty experience for two such gentle parents. But in the long run it was far nastier for James than it was for them. Their troubles were all over in a jiffy.

They were dead and gone in thirty-five seconds flat. Poor James, on the other hand, was still very much alive, and all at once he found himself alone and frightened in a vast unfriendly world" (Dahl, 1961, p. 2). Dahl's descriptions of the two selfish aunts, Aunt Sponge and Aunt Spiker, and their abuse of James are vivid and the prose quickly captivates readers. Could it be that Dahl was speaking, at least partially, from experience? Roald Dahl was sent to boarding school at the young age of 8. He spent 10 years in an academic environment that he clearly hated. In Dahl's words, "Those were days of horror, of fierce discipline, of no talking in the dormitories, no running in the corridors, no untidiness of any sort, no this or that or the other, just rules, rules and still more rules that had to be obeyed. And the fear of the dreaded cane hung over us like the fear of death all the time" (Trelease, 1992, p.298). It is interesting to consider the mean and hateful descriptions of the two aunts alongside Dahl's description of his schooling experiences. You can't always assume that the author's real-life experiences are the basis for his or her fiction, but doesn't it make you wonder whether Aunt Sponge and Aunt Spiker were inspired by Dahl's own experiences? It is also interesting to look at any of Dahl's children's books, and even some adult short stories, and notice the playful, mischievous tones in his books. It's as if he wants children to celebrate childhood, run in the corridors, and break free of purposeless "rules, rules and still more rules." Dahl may have passed away in 1990, but he still very much lives within his books.

⚙ Listening for Bias

Just as there is a personal stamp on Dahl's work, the same is true for nonfiction and informational texts. It is highly unlikely that an author would feel compelled to write an informational piece with which he or she disagrees. Writing well requires inspiration. It has to be felt. Even informational pieces carry traces of their authors and evidence into their experiences, worldviews, and beliefs. This is known as the author's bias. It's important that students know this. We need to help them to objectively critique works based on not only what is within the text, but also why the author felt compelled to put certain things within the text. Students need to be able to critique the credibility of the piece based on any known biases. If we separate the work from its author, we risk missing important opportunities for higher-order analysis of the text and what is contained within it. And we risk seeing only part of the story and therefore being unable to critique the overall credibility of the message. Adolescence provides a perfect time for students to be introduced to bias.

It's important for students to begin to realize that even nonfiction holds the author's opinion, even if it is cushioned in fact.

Asking the students to read portions of texts out loud after they've read the words silently can lead to some very interesting perspectives. Did the author sound angry? What made the text sound as though the author was angry? Did the author speak with a sense of urgency, or with a calm but sad sense of reflection? Consider the words that we wrote earlier, in the section titled "A Tale of Two Countries." In particular, consider the final sentence: "Reading Toscana's passionate rant, in light of the data on the declining levels of leisure reading in the United States, we couldn't help but wonder if, to a certain extent, we weren't also reading the words of the Ghost of Christmas Future." What were the emotions ascribed? What in the text makes you think that? What other clues can be found within that section that divulge a little about our beliefs and values? All authors, or at least most, whether they intend to or not, eventually give themselves away by what they write and how they write it. Helping students explore that reality is an essential part of their development as critical thinkers.

⚙ Critiquing the Message via Multiple Perspectives

Words are powerful. Throughout history, unimaginable atrocities have been committed, in many cases, because leaders have been able to effectively convince the majority using powerful and poisonous words. Our children need to become geniuses at seeing through the power of words, to question, to critically analyze and evaluate what they are reading, so that well-articulated but poorly grounded arguments will garner more critical attention. We need to teach them how to think critically. Often, the best way to do that is to rely on varying, and oftentimes conflicting, accounts on the same issue. Eighth grade English teacher Matt Baker used three different sources in order to provide depth to the concepts of emigration and immigration. In addition to the core text, *Across America on an Emigrant Train* (Murphy, 2003), Baker also added the short story "First Crossing" by Pam Munoz Ryan (in Gallo, 2007), which tells the contemporary story of a teenage immigrant boy and the risks involved with being smuggled across the Mexican border. The students also analyzed one of more than 100 poems carved on one of the wooden walls of Angel Island's Immigration Station's detention barracks in San Francisco (*Encouraging the Traveler* by Xu from Xianshan). Students compared and contrasted the experiences of the various immigration stories.

According to Baker, "Overall, many students looked at the book, the poem, and the short story and groaned. By the end, those same students were asking questions faster than I could possibly respond. They connected to Robert Louis Stevenson's leaving home, disappointing his parents, all for love of a 'forbidden woman.' They know that Marco and his father are breaking the law in crossing the border, but we looked at the situation from multiple points of view and researched our own border issues. The pairing of three texts was truly difficult, but in the end the connections students were able to make offered far more depth of understanding than if we had simply read one text." High school English teacher and curricular leader David Vega also uses multiple sources to help students gain deeper perspectives about issues contained within core texts. According to Vega, "I help students acquire the requisite context and background, except not through passive PowerPoints or lectures; students instead read controversial news, human interest stories, or reference articles that help them build background for accessing the target text. Many times, the selections are differentiated. Struggling readers will work with selections that are less complex than the target text, while strong readers will work with grade-level selections. Students annotate, question, and discuss the background text. Then I ask them to take a position regarding something controversial in the text. They write persuasively before we debate. This is how I squeeze many nonfiction pieces into literature units."

⚙ Reading as Skeptics

Author and award-winning teacher Larry Ferlazzo hosted several guests on his EdWeek blog. He asked them to address the question of how to deal with history myths in the classroom (blog appeared in Classroom Q & A, on Jan. 12, 2013). Their responses were powerful. Teacher leader Stephen Lazar responded, "The most destructive myth is that 'history is simple.' In an effort to be comprehensible, textbooks too often take complex causations and individuals and turn them into neatly identifiable causes and caricatures." Lazar's solution to the linear treatments and the lack of complexities inherent in texts is to bring in other sources. According to Lazar, "My first step in combating this problem is simple: I don't use a textbook. Rather, students read collections of primary documents that help them discover these complexities. Students then read multiple secondary sources that offer competing narratives, so that they learn that different historians create different interpretations while they are also equipped with primary source information to create their own interpretations."

ASCD author ReLeah Cossent Lent addressed Ferlazzo's prompt with a similar emphasis on the need for a critical look at multiple sources. Though her response did not completely eliminate the use of the textbook, she emphasized the need to help students read textbooks and other sources with a critical eye. According to Cossent Lent, "the very nature of history requires that students read as skeptics, question the motivations of the writer, dig into primary documents, compare perspectives, and come to understand that history is a mirror that reflects many different faces . . . . History teachers dispel this myth by engaging students in multiple texts of various genres and formats as they encourage thoughtful reading and active discussion. Such teachers help students develop the questioning stance of historians instead of the robotic 'read to find the answer' habits many students have perfected."

In response to the same prompt, *Rethinking Schools* magazine editor Bill Bigelow wrote that "there are countless things wrong with having textbooks play a major role in the school curriculum: they seek to avoid controversy; they embed a worldview consistent with that of the giant for-profit corporations that produce them; they hand students conclusions rather than dilemmas, supposed facts rather than choices; they make social change appear to be the product of Great Individuals rather than social movements; and through their silence about so many important issues, textbooks inure students to the crises that influence the kind of lives they will lead."

When teaching anything, and history in particular, we need to rely on more than the canned answers that are readily offered to us in our packaged curricula. The biggest problems with relying solely on a packaged text is that we perpetuate myths. We'd like to revisit some of what we feel were the most powerful statements in Ferlazzo's blog regarding these myths and the short-comings of a one-text based curriculum. "The most destructive myth is that 'history is simple" (Lazar). "The very nature of history requires that students read as skeptics" (Cossent Lent). And finally, "they hand students conclusions rather than dilemmas" (Bigelow). Though, as noted by Matt Baker, finding multiple sources may be time-consuming, it leads to wonderfully rich learning opportunities that are much deeper than what might have been experienced by solely relying on one text.

⚙ Finding Relevance

Third grade teachers Krista Grimm and Susan Hagel were surprised to find out that their students, the majority of whom are Puerto Rican, had never heard of Puerto Rican baseball legend Roberto Clemente. Not only had they not heard of him, but the students were also unaware that the local park, just blocks away, had been named in honor of Roberto Clemente. In addition to the text that they had planned to read on this topic, Grimm and Hagel compiled several resources, including various texts, pictures of the park, and an audiobook on Roberto Clemente read by a Spanish-speaking author who still retained the Spanish accent familiar to so many of the students. Little by little they began helping the students make connections regarding their own lives, Roberto Clemente's life, and the role of baseball—which remains a dearly loved sport to so many Puerto Ricans and to several of the students in this 3rd grade class. With each exploration, students became more invested. During one shared reading experience, Hagel recounts, "They kept getting up on their knees. They were so engaged and focused. They were the most engaged I've ever seen them." By the time the students were presented with their writing tasks, Grimm noted, "This was the best writing I have seen all year, because they were so into it. Even my student who came to the States only a year ago—he was so into the book that he did his writing independently." Helping students see the relevance in what they will be reading or writing about is a powerful motivator in helping them succeed.

⚙ The Relevance Wheel

The Relevance Wheel (Himmele & Himmele, 2009, p.62) offers opportunities for students to make connections between what they are learning and how it affects them and the world around them. Though the Relevance Wheel lends itself well to teaching history, it can also apply to many of the informational texts that students are required to read in other content areas. The student sample provided in Figure 3.4 is a Relevance Wheel on the scientific topic of hurricanes. Figure 3.5 presents a template with six inner spokes. Students write down the concepts they learned on the spokes. On the outer wheel, students then address how it affects them and the world around them. Typically, completing the Relevance Wheel does require some modeling, especially the first time it is completed. But once students know how to fill one out, the template can be used to address many of the themes that have a palpable impact

Figure 3.4

Claire and Gabriela's Hurricane Relevance Wheel

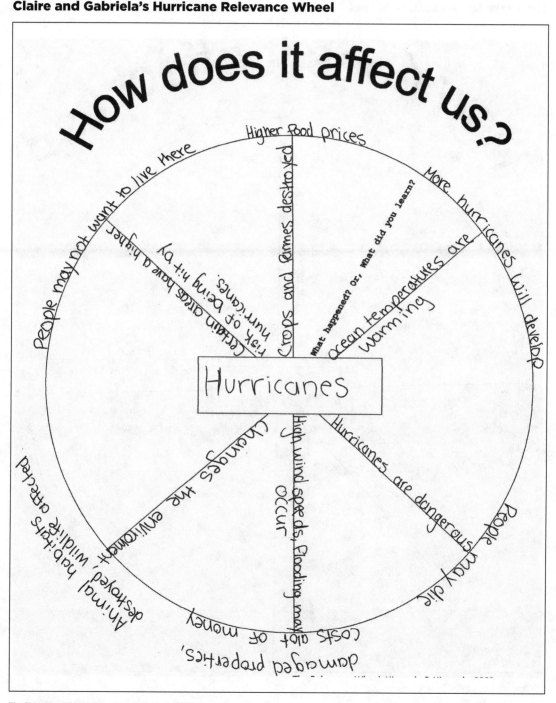

The Relevance Wheel, Himmele and Himmele, 2009.

Figure 3.5

Template for Relevance Wheel

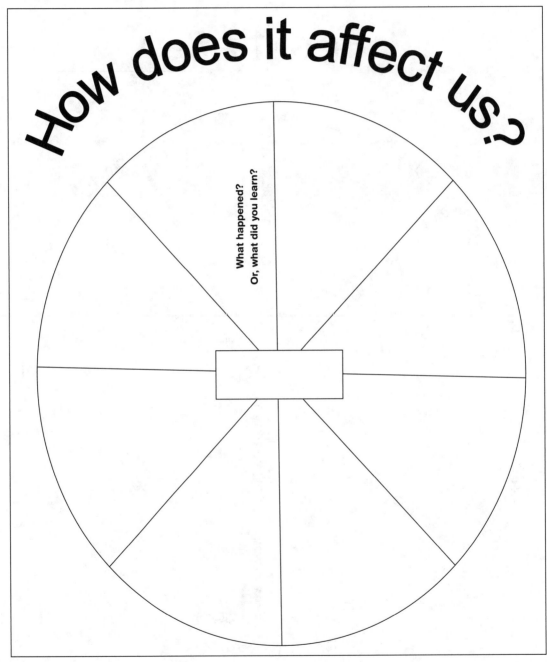

The Relevance Wheel, Himmele and Himmele, 2009.

on society, and it can be used to help students make the connections between what they are learning and how it affects the world around them.

⚙ What's It *Really* About?

One of the ways that Keely Potter gets her students to jump to the overall picture and relevance of the subject that they are reading about is a simple exaggerated emphasis that she places on the word *really*. She begins by asking students, "All right, what's it about?" Once students respond, she then asks. "All right, but what's it *reeeeeeaaally* about?" Because of her exaggerated emphasis, her students know that she is no longer asking them for a literal interpretation—she now wants them to analyze the hidden messages, the author's intent, and the relevance regarding what was written. Figure 3.6 is meant to allow students to respond to these prompts in an individual quick-write format, so that by the time the question is asked of the whole group, each student will have already thought about it.

Figure 3.6

Quick-Write Template for "What's It *Really* About?"

Name_____ Date _____
What's it about?
What's it *reeeeaally* about?

Conclusion

Content knowledge will only take students so far. But how students use, synthesize, and contend with that content knowledge is what will really matter in terms of helping to support students on their paths to becoming world change makers. Our classrooms are opportunities for opening minds, not just filling them. When we come to even a tiny realization of the incredible potential within each of our students, and the impact that each can have on our world once they've left our classrooms, it sheds a greater importance on the process of thinking about concepts rather than simply learning concepts. Why? Who cares? How can I use this? What am I noticing here? How can I make this better? These are the types of questions that empower students not just to know content but to affect it, and to affect the world through it.

We have had many wonderful opportunities to travel to numerous countries throughout the world. We've been invited into classrooms and have been introduced to students in elementary as well as secondary settings, many of which, at least in appearances, have seemed to be working at what we would deem remarkably "above grade level." Yet, we are convinced, now more than ever, that what matters most in creating long-term impact is not how much children learn but what they are prepared to do with what they learn, and the boldness with which they analyze, synthesize, and dare to question what they are learning. These are the students who can change the world. These are the students who are in your classrooms.

4

Tools for Supporting Literary Analysis

I was reading and connecting. I was so into the book that I lost track of time. —Phillip, 6th grade

Effective Readers and Writers

It goes without saying that in order to be college- and career-ready, students will need to become effective readers and writers. In the long run, the skills needed to succeed with highly sophisticated college-level texts and the expectations for deep levels of understanding will require a sustained focus on developing active, critical readers and writers throughout students' K–12 experiences. This chapter provides suggestions, strategies, and tools for helping students in grades 3 through 12 become active and critical readers.

⚙ Reader Surveys

Before helping students progress, it is important to know who your students are and what they need. While there are numerous standardized and commercial assessments that provide a picture of a student's application of reading skills at a given moment in time, these assessments often fail to capture some of the most important affective and qualitative data regarding the students' development, perceptions, attitudes, and approaches toward reading. Some of this rich data can be obtained by asking the students pointed questions that tell you about their development as readers. Documenting students' responses and comparing them over time can give you a road map of how the student's perceptions, attitudes, and approaches are changing. Helping the students to evaluate

Tools and Techniques Included in This Chapter:

- Reader Surveys
- Reading Conference Question Bank
- Monitoring Independent Work
- Recording Your Reading History
- Reading Response Tool Sheets
- Book Talks
- Processing Bookmark
- Exploring Genres— Passports
- Collecting Words Wall
- Great Opening Lines Wall
- Great One-Liners Wall
- Genre Wall
- The Class Bookworm
- The WIDU Board

their own growth by comparing their own responses over time can also help students take ownership of the process of their own reading development. Figure 4.1 provides sample survey questions that might be asked of students at periodic intervals. These surveys can be administered every few months or once a marking period. It is amazing how much valuable data can be obtained from the student surveys. They can help you develop focused action plans as a direct response to your students' needs.

Figure 4.1
Reader Surveys

Name_____ Date _____

1. What have you been reading?

2. Describe your story as a reader. When did you first become a reader? If you've already answered this question in former surveys, talk about how you have recently seen yourself grow or change as a reader.

3. In terms of reading, in what areas would you like to see yourself grow?

4. Tell me about your experiences reading fiction. Are you successful with reading fiction? Why or why not?

5. Tell me about your experiences reading nonfiction and informational texts. Are you successful with reading nonfiction and informational texts? Why or why not?

6. Are you noticing new vocabulary as you read? Are you noticing growth in your vocabulary as you read? Please elaborate (tell me more).

7. Overall, as a learner, with what do you feel confident and with what are you still struggling?

8. What strategies do we use in class, or which ones have you developed, that are helping you develop as a reader and as a learner?

9. What do I (or other teachers) do that helps you learn better?

10. Is there anything else you'd like to say about reading? If so, write it here. If there is a question you think I should have asked, please share it here.

By Pérsida and William Himmele.

⚙ Reading Conference Question Bank

Individual student conferences are critical for helping students progress, as well as for constantly revisiting where students are on their learning continua. In addition to helping you gather information regarding reading progress, reading conferences also go a long way in building relationships and in helping you know who your students are. Reading conferences can be conducted while students are engaging in silent reading or other individual assignments. Once the school year is underway, a brief but effective reading conference can take less than five minutes. They can play an important role in helping teachers gather information regarding each student's success with self-selected independent reading, as well as with teacher-selected books and informational texts. Many students really benefit from this face-to-face individualized interaction. When 7th grader Ridge was asked to explain what his teacher did that helped the most in his literacy development, he answered, "[She] talked to us one-on-one, because I do better when it's just the teacher and me."

A brief template for the suggested reading conference prompts is included in Figure 4.2. Rather than ask all of the questions in Figure 4.2, select the ones that you believe will best inform you of each student's progress. The more often you conference and jot down anecdotal notes, the better you'll know your students, and the better you will be able to influence your students' growth. Figure 4.3 is an example of how teachers might record information from reading conferences. If you have 25 students, it would mean you'd need a stapled pad of 25 of these, so that you can simply flip to the name of the student with whom you are conferencing and record highlights of your conference as it is happening. By having one student's notes dedicated to each page, you'll be able to more easily see progress over time while also conferencing with some students more than others. Making double-sided copies, where each student is given the two-sided sheet, would increase the amount of use you could get from each pad without having to add more sheets.

⚙ Monitoring Independent Work

In addition to making sure that conferences go well, it is also important that teachers be able to monitor the progress of the students working independently. How teachers monitor and document the conferences and independent work can make a critical difference in whether or not the conferences will be both practical and useful. Conferences can be conducted while students are

Figure 4.2

Reading Conference Question Bank

Reading Conferences

Literature

1. Tell me about the book you are reading.

2. Is it going well? Why or why not?

3. Which of the Elements of Fiction are drawing you in. With which are you struggling? (For younger children, the Elements of Fiction can be spelled out to focus on the ones that have been taught. Elements of Fiction include setting, characters, plot, exposition, rising action, climax, falling action, resolution, themes, style, and symbolism.)

4. Read me the excerpt that you selected to focus on. (Prior to the conference, ask students to select an excerpt on which to focus.)

5. What made you select that excerpt? How does the author use words to achieve his or her purpose?

6. Tell me about the new vocabulary you encountered.

Informational Text

7. How are you doing with reading informational texts?

8. Describe for me your most recent experiences reading informational text. What worked for you? What are you still working on?

9. Tell me about how you attack a text. Tell me about how you make sense of it and what features help you.

10. Tell me about your successes.

11. With what kinds of things are you struggling?

Overall

12. Tell me about your overall reading experiences since we last talked.

13. Show me how you have been keeping track of your thinking (notes, processing bookmarks, post-its, etc.).

14. Tell me about any reading goals you're working toward with regard to literature and/or informational texts.

By Pérsida and William Himmele.

reading independently, completing readers' responses, or writing. Whatever students are doing, it is critical that teachers develop an effective system of monitoring all students' work and documenting the information gathered during the reading conferences. Figure 4.4 provides a quick accountability tool for helping those that are working independently to document their work. Before starting the reading conferences, students can be assigned their tasks and they can fill out the start time and the goal on the template. Once conferences are completed for the day, students can then fill in the progress made and the end time, and either submit it to the teacher or have it out and ready for a quick review while the teacher quickly walks around the room reviewing the work logs,

Figure 4.3

Sample Record Keeping Sheet for Reading Conferences
(one double-sided sheet per student)

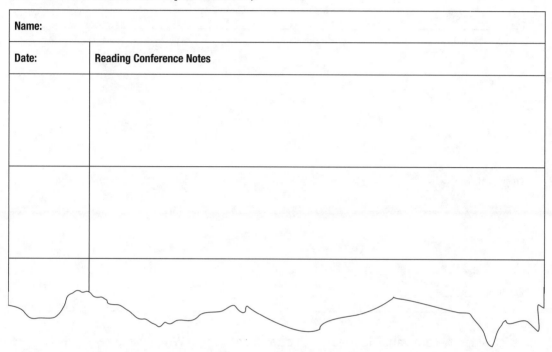

Name:	
Date:	Reading Conference Notes

or students can keep it in an independent work log that can be reviewed at a more convenient time.

Finding Your Literary Soul Mate

Many of Potter's students come to her with little affection for reading. So developing positive affective components of reading is a critical ingredient in helping her students become avid readers. Potter often refers to *The Book* as that one book that will make students fall in love with reading. Students will often hear Potter encourage them that if they haven't found it already, there exists a type of literary soul mate that contains just the right elements of fiction to draw them in. In order to make students more aware of these elements, her reading conferences will prompt students to discuss the elements that they liked or didn't like within the books that they read. The quest to find a literary soul mate, or *The Book*, is something that Potter never gives up on, and students knew what we meant when we asked them about *The Book*. Ninth grader

Figure 4.4

Independent Work Log

Independent Work Log

Name:_____ Date:_____

Start Time:_____

Goal:

Progress Made:

End Time:_____

Ian became an avid reader in Potter's classroom. When we asked him about *The Book*, he responded, "I was entranced by *The Book*. As a reader I noticed myself shredding it apart. Analyzing and processing the words that were on the page before me, like I've never done before, piecing together the puzzle that was *The Book*. My skills as a reader increased drastically, more than I could've ever thought possible. As a reader, I noticed myself improving."

Jaycie explained what she noticed after she found the right book. "When I was reading in 5th grade it was like watching a movie. I could tell what was happening. Before that, I didn't feel like reading was my thing." It is important to note the process involved a faithfulness to the read-aloud and the subsequent book-based think-alouds. In our own experiences, we have found that a strong independent reading component paired with a strong read-aloud component is essential in helping students want to find and read *The Book*. The read-aloud provides the incentive and allows students to see the type of mind-movie to which Jaycie referred. It helps them appreciate the potential benefits that can be gained from reading a good book. Without read-alouds, many students are left with little incentive to clumsily plod through books, struggling with issues related to fluency, comprehension, and overall reading skill development that impede their enjoyment. Surrounded by read-alouds, they'll want to take the time to get better at reading, because they know how good it can be.

During our interviews, students remembered, with seeming affection, when they came across *The Book*. For some students, finding that book took years of being in Potter's class. Seventh grade Tanner was an example of that. According to Potter, "Tanner had picked up every book in the classroom library, and he'd bring it back 1/4 read, and say, 'This isn't gonna work for me. It's not my book'. And I'd say, 'But Tanner, why isn't it your book?' We'd talk about why he didn't like it. This year, Tanner finally found his book. It was a series and he was just addicted to the stories. But it took three years for him to find his book. I never stoppped telling him that he could find it. I never told him he could stop trying." We also interviewed a few students who couldn't recall which book was *The Book*. These were typically the students who had found the love of reading early in life. For 9th grader Kinsey, every book is *The Book:* "Each book holds a different puzzle piece to the mirror of me, and I still have a lot more pieces to find." We could go on and on regaling touching stories of how students affectionately referred to their finding *The Book*. One thing was clear: each story held within it a testament to the power of good books in developing avid readers, and the power of teachers who change lives forever by helping students find their literary soul mates.

⚙ Recording Your Reading History

In a lesson plan posted in the *New York Times'* Learning Network, authors Brown and Schulten (2010) explore the power of helping students revisit their personal histories with literature. Their lesson plan provides the nuts and bolts for helping students visualize their first experiences with literacy through their current standings with literacy, and then recording these using tools such as time lines. Edutopia blogger Sara Mulhern Gross (2013) expanded this concept into having students create infographics of their time lines. Her blog includes a picture of an infographic that chronicles one high school student's literary journey starting with the Junie B. Jones series in kindergarten, through the worst book she had ever read, onto the beloved Hunger Games series—which helped her identify symbolism in literature—to her current encounters with the world via *Time* magazine. It is a beautiful project that captures the power of literacy in shaping who we are and how we think. The URLs for both of these sources can be found in our reference list. We encourage you to examine these for visuals and templates that can help capture your students' reading histories.

⚙ Reading Response Tool Sheets

In contrast to the students who have little affection for reading, you will likely come across students who have a great affection for reading, but who fail to read critically or who have no desire to stop and demonstrate their ability to analyze what they are reading. Eighth grader Alexis developed a deep love for reading and began reading everything that she could get her hands on within her favorite genre. According to Alexis, "I see books in a totally different way now. I even got a membership at Books-A-Million, and if I had a ton of money, I would buy every book in that place. Before, I wouldn't have even gone in that place." Alexis loved reading so much that at home she was grounded from reading because she wasn't getting her content homework finished. Her leisure reading books had to be confiscated until after she completed all of her content work. But while her teacher, Keely Potter, noticed that she had devoured book after book, she also noticed that Alexis wasn't transferring her new-found reading fluency, comprehension, and love for reading into the ability to analyze her texts or less enjoyable content material, nonfiction, or works that had been selected for the purpose of literary analysis. According to Potter, "She found the love of reading and would prefer to read for enjoyment versus the analysis needed for responding to readings. And even though she was very capable, her love of reading wasn't transferring into being able to demonstrate that she could analyze what she was reading. She didn't want to have to work hard. She just wanted to read, read, read. My feedback kept pointing her to the tool sheets. She followed the tool sheets and finally wrote that masterpiece reading response." Potter's direct feedback, as well as tool sheet prompts that focused on analysis rather than retelling, are what supported Alexis in moving from lower-order thinking to higher-order thinking. Figures 4.5, 4.6, and 4.7 provide reading reponse tool sheets that can help you move your students from literal understandings to higher-order understandings of what they read. They are written for three developmental levels—the early intermediate grades (approximately grades 3 to 5), the intermediate and middle school grades (approximately grades 5 to 8), and the middle and high school grades (approximately grades 7 to 12). Read through them to decide which best fits the students whom you teach.

Figure 4.5
Stage 1 Reading Response Tool Sheet

Reading Response Tool Sheet (Stage 1: Early Intermediate Grades)

Name_____ Date _____

Ideas

- ☐ Did I explain what the book is about?
- ☐ Did I select my favorite parts and tell why they are my favorite parts?
- ☐ Did I provide specific *examples* that show how the character changed in the story? (Note: You must cite, using quotation marks and page numbers.)
- ☐ Did I provide specific *examples* of how the author used words to make me like or dislike characters, or feel worry or other emotions? (Note: You must cite, using quotation marks and page numbers.)
- ☐ Did I discuss the ending and how I reacted to it as the reader? (This is for written responses only. Do not share the ending if you are doing a Book Talk.)
- ☐ Did I talk about the genre and the perfect audience for this book?

Editing

Organization

- ☐ Did I include an opening paragraph that introduces the book and an overview of what I will be writing about?
- ☐ Did I include a concluding paragraph that sums up how I feel about this book and discusses the genre and the perfect audience for this book?

Sentence Fluency

- ☐ Did I read my paper out loud and slowly? Do the sentences sound right?

Voice and Word Choice

- ☐ Did I take a risk and include new or interesting words?

I am most proud of my use of these words:

_____

I am most proud of this sentence:

_____

Conventions

- ☐ Do I have evidence that I have edited and revised my reading response, so that it does not contain distracting typos and mistakes? Submit first and final drafts together.

Adapted by Pérsida and William Himmele from Keely Potter's Reading Response Tool Sheets. Used with permission.

Figure 4.6

Stage 2 Reading Response Tool Sheet

Reading Response Tool Sheet (Stage 2: Intermediate & Middle School Grades)

Name_____ Date _____

Ideas

☐ Did I include enough about the plot so that the reader can understand the important developments and the major conflict (including the rising action, climax, and falling action)?

☐ Did I provide specific examples that show how the character changed in the story?

☐ Did I provide specific examples that show how the changed character was affected by other characters? (protagonist/antagonist)

☐ Did I discuss underlying issues that develop throughout the text? Are there connections to real life, other books, or my own experiences that demonstrate that certain themes are developing?

☐ Did I discuss how the author used words to set a tone in the book?

☐ Did I discuss the ending and how I reacted to it as the reader? (This is for written responses only. Do not share the ending if you are doing a Book Talk.)

☐ Did I talk about why I think the book fits within a certain genre, and what Elements of Fiction make this book fit under a certain genre? Did I talk about the intended audience for this book, and what makes me think that the author wrote this for that target audience?

☐ Did I read the Higher-Order Thinking chart to help me remember the type of thinking that is being expected of me?

Editing

Organization

☐ Does my reading response have a logical organization? Is it easy for the reader to follow?

Sentence Fluency

☐ Did I read my paper out loud and slowly? Do the sentences sound right?

Voice and Word Choice

☐ Am I developing my voice? Do I choose words that set a certain tone? Does my tone lead to an overall mood in my Reading Response? I've selected five words that give this Reading Response a character that is intentional and uniquely "Me":

_____

Conventions

☐ Do I have evidence that I have edited and revised my reading response, so that it does not contain distracting typos and mistakes? Submit first and final drafts together.

Adapted by Pérsida and William Himmele from Keely Potter's Reading Response Tool Sheets. Used with permission.

Figure 4.7
Stage 3 Reading Response Tool Sheet

Reading Response Tool Sheet (Stage 3: Middle & High School Grades)

Name_____ Date _____

Ideas
The Elements of Fiction refer to things like setting, characters, plot, exposition, rising action, climax, falling action, resolution, themes, style, and symbolism.

☐ Did I provide a picture of how the author develops Elements of Fiction within the text?

☐ Which Elements of Fiction did I choose to discuss? (Or, which Elements was I asked to discuss):

_____

_____

☐ Did I attempt to analyze the Elements of Fiction rather than just label them?

☐ Did I provide examples of how certain Elements of Fiction affect each other and how they are affected by each other?

☐ Did I provide text-based evidence, cited in quotation marks, along with page numbers for what I analyzed?

☐ Did I talk about why I think the book fits within a certain genre, and what Elements of Fiction make this book fit within this genre? Did I talk about the intended audience for this book and what makes me think that the author wrote this for that target audience?

☐ Did I read the Higher-Order Thinking chart to help me remember the type of thinking that is being expected of me?

Editing

Organization

☐ Does my reading response have a logical organization? Is it easy for the reader to follow?

Sentence Fluency

☐ Are my sentences varied in their length, complexity, and construction?

☐ Did I read my paper out loud and slowly? Do the sentences sound right?

Voice and Word Choice

☐ Am I developing my voice? Do I choose words that set a certain tone? Does my tone lead to an overall mood in my Reading Response? I've selected five words that give this Reading Response a character that is intentional and uniquely "Me":

_____

Conventions

☐ Do I have evidence that I have edited and revised my reading response, so that it does not contain distracting typos and mistakes? Submit first and final drafts together.

Adapted by Pérsida and William Himmele from Keely Potter's Reading Response Tool Sheets. Used with permission.

⚙ Book Talks

Book talks are oral presentations of student's reading responses. Lasting anywhere from three to five minutes, book talks differ from reading responses only in that students are asked not to share the ending of the book. This allows students to take a break from writing reading responses, while still requiring them to analyze the books. Book talks require that students address the components found on the Reading Response Tool Sheets, but the students present their analyses with an emphasis on grabbing other readers' attention.

Teachers can also allow students to create artistic expressions of their books, which are coupled with a book talk and which serve to enhance the book talk. Seventh grader Jaycie created a bulletin-board-sized wall display dedicated to Kate DiCamillo's *The Tale of Desperaux* (2003). According to Jaycie, "I didn't think that I could represent that book well by just writing it." She used colors to represent specific major themes in the book. For Jaycie, the project allowed her to express her thoughts about the different themes and the interconnectedness of the four sections of DiCamillo's book in a much better way than if she had been required to write about it first. She believes that the project can actually serve as a writing scaffold. According to Jaycie, "As far as writing my project, I don't like to write. I feel able to write more when I get these feelings out. Like I could look at my *Tale of Desperaux* project, and probably write two or three pages on it now. So I feel like if teachers let kids get their ideas out, and let them look at it, I think that teachers would be surprised at how much better kids could write."

⚙ Processing Bookmark

Legare (2012) found that students learn better when they are asked to explain their thinking. Furthermore, when students were asked to explain inconsistencies, it led them to further investigate their responses, thereby supporting their learning (Legare, Schepp & Gelman, 2014). This metacognitive processing is also important when students are reading. It also prepares them to talk about their books. Keeping track of one's own thinking is an important metacognitive process that prepares students to talk and write about what they are reading. While students may not enjoy interrupting their reading to write notes, the process can actually support their ability to demonstrate their ability to analyze what they read. Figure 4.8 provides a sample of a Processing Bookmark that students can keep within their books to jot down notes as they read. Students can also use Post-its or other note-taking tools. The important thing is that they be able to provide evidence that they are analyzing and processing what they are reading.

Figure 4.8
Processing Thinking Bookmark

Processing Bookmark

Keep track of your thinking by recording your **analysis** of what you are reading, along with the **page number.**
Refer to the Higher-Order Thinking chart for a description of analysis.

⚙ Exploring Genres—Passports

Exploring different genres with students can be a challenging proposition that can lead to some uncomfortable choices. If understanding the differences in genre is important, should we then force students to put down their current favorites in exchange for exploring books across genres? If all students ever read are *Captain Underpants* books, will they ever acquire the academic language that is so critically important to their success in school? Honoring student choices is an important part of helping them become avid readers. We believe that students' independent reading times ought to be reserved for student self-selected books in whatever genres they prefer. Exposure to texts across different genres is a different matter altogether. In-class teacher-facilitated reading time is where students can be effectively exposed to books across genres, and opportunities to compare and analyze features specific to genres. It also helps encourage students to branch out into other genres by exposing them to books within these new genres.

Carmen Rowe and Jessica Bamberger have had a great deal of success in getting students to explore other genres by simply addressing students' choices in books during reading conferences. Rowe keeps track of students' independent reading books on charts within their portfolios. These charts provide the tools that she uses to have deeper heart-to-heart conversations. Because she works with English language learners, increasing the level of linguistic and cognitive complexity in books that are read is an important part of accelerating language development. But at the same time, she doesn't want to lose students by forcing them to read books that they don't want to read. Rowe's conferencing oftentimes results in students making the effort to explore books in different genres with different levels of linguistic complexities. Through conferencing, she finds students become interested in other types of books if they are given enough of a tantalizing description beforehand. All the while, students still maintain a love for literature. Fourth grade teacher Jessica Bamberger created a Genre Passport that celebrates whenever students "travel to a different country" by reading within a new genre. The passports provide a nice reference tool that helps students quickly see their reading history for the year and how each of those books fit within a different genre.

Student-generated classroom displays

In this section, we'd like to propose various interactive displays that rely on student contributions. It might be a bulletin board set aside for students to add to, or it can be as simple as a piece of chart paper or butcher paper with a title prompt selected by the teacher and a blank space for students to write on.

⚙ Collecting Words Wall

Ask students to keep track of vocabulary they have learned. For example, they can keep track of new, beautiful, or unusual words in their readings using the collecting words bookmarks presented earlier (Figure 2.1). When they come across vocabulary words or interesting words in their readings, ask students to add them to an index card or the template in Figure 4.9, explain the meaning, illustrate it, and attach it to the Collecting Words Wall. Periodically revisit the display by asking students to spend some time reading the entries or creating categories about the entries. For example, what is a sentence that captures the types of words that students found interesting? How can the words be categorized? What parts of speech were represented by most of the student-selected words?

Figure 4.9
Collecting Words Template for Collecting Words Wall

Name_____ **Date**_____
Where did you come across the word?_____
Choice word (write this in marker, so that it's visible from far away):
What does it mean and how was it used? (Write this in pen or pencil.)   Add a picture that captures its meaning.

Great Opening Lines Wall

Many people who have never even read Charles Dickens's 1859 classic, *A Tale of Two Cities*, can still identify his great opening line: "It was the best of times, it was the worst of times." Or how about this great opening line that immediately sets readers up for the tongue-in-cheek humor they will no doubt find peppered throughout the descriptions within the book: "It is a truth universally acknowledged, that a single man in possession of a good fortune, must be in want of a wife" (Jane Austen, *Pride and Prejudice* 1813). Can great books even become great books without great opening lines? Though we are not sure that this question can be answered, there is no doubt that a great opening line helps build anticipation in the reader and helps establish the mood that something really fabulous is about to be read.

With this wall, dedicated to great opening lines, you'll help readers celebrate their discoveries of ways that authors prepare readers to enter into a wonderful literary experience through the author's artistry of words. Ask students to be alert to ways that authors begin books, chapters, or poetry. Whenever they come across a great opening line, they should add it to the display. They could add these lines directly to a piece of chart paper dedicated for this purpose or use the template in Figure 4.10. This display reminds students of how authors use great opening lines to draw readers in. Teachers and students can make reference to this display when they need examples of how authors use words to immediately hook readers. If you really want to analyze both sides of the opening line equation, a portion of the display can be set up to explore not-so-great opening lines.

Great One-Liners Wall

A variation of the Great Opening Lines Wall would be to have a Great One-Liners Wall, where students record favorite lines that capture deep meanings or that set a certain mood. Ninth grader Kinsey wrote, "In every book that I have come to love, there are different one-liners that catch my eye. These words or phrases may be something as simple as something I don't know. But usually, these one-liners are things that make me stop and think, 'I connect to this.'" Further elaborations on this concept can expand to displays dedicated to *metaphors* and *symbolism,* encouraging students to stop and notice these within their texts and then celebrate these by posting them on the display.

Figure 4.10

Great Opening Lines Template

Name _____ Date _____

Title _____

Author _____

Great Opening Line:

What makes it a great opening line?

(Post this on the wall, but don't forget to come back and finish this part after you read the book/text.) Did the book/text live up to its great opening line? Why or why not?

⚙ Genre Wall

When students collectively share their reading journeys, the community of students begins to know who likes what genre and make genre-based recommendations. In the same vein as the other displays, students can use this dedicated spot to recommend books based on specific genres. The display can be set up so that the genre titles are moveable; in the event that certain genres receive fewer recommendations, they can be moved and reattached elsewhere on the display to make room for the genres that are more popular.

⚙ The Class Bookworm

You will probably find that students will likely want to read popular fiction or nonfiction based on personal preferences without the commitment of writing a reader response. The bookworm is a tool that provides a less formal venue for students to share their thoughts related to books they've read, and it makes a nice supplement to literary analysis. When teaching reading to 6th graders, coauthor Pérsida Himmele put up a bookworm head made out of green and white construction paper. Students would then voluntarily complete book reviews that were never edited or graded, and that served as a way of recommending or warning peers about books. The completed book reviews were attached to backgrounds of green precut construction paper circles that were attached to the wall, becoming the bookworm's body segments.

During independent reading times, every breathing soul in the room had to have a book open and be reading it, including Pérsida. It was an uninterrupted sacred time that she and her students came to love. Other than silently reading during that time, students were allowed to take a break and provide a written book review that would be attached to a green precut bookworm segment. At the end of independent reading time, those who had completed a book review could attach their reviews to the classroom bookworm. The feedback was revisited when Pérsida would ask students to share their reviews with the class. By the end of the year, the bookworm swirled and looped from one end of the classroom through all four walls, ending where the head met the final segment. Every student had voluntarily (some with encouragement) contributed approximately 10 nongraded, no-credit-given segments to the classroom bookworm. While the book reviews come nowhere near the level of analysis inherent in formal reading responses, they do provide a nongraded supplement for when students simply want to informally talk about a book.

⚙ The WIDU Board

Small-group discussions can often lead to unanswered student questions regarding the topic being discussed. High school English teacher Brandon Bailey found a convenient solution to addressing these questions using a bulletin board with the letters *WIDU*, which stand for *What I Don't Understand*. On this student-generated bulletin board, students post their questions on index cards. Bailey addresses these questions in class, opening it up so that peers can respond to one another's questions. The bulletin board has had several benefits in terms of giving students control over their own learning. According to Bailey, "The original idea behind the WIDU board was essentially a collection of questions the students came up with. By getting them involved and having classmates try to answer the question, I had little to clean up in terms of questions I wanted to cover in class." Providing a place where students can post their questions allows students to be heard, even when they don't feel comfortable asking questions out loud. It also prevents students from forgetting their question, eliminates

Figure 4.11
Bookworm Review

Bookworm Review by: _____ Date: _____
Title and author:
Without giving away the ending, give us a feel for what the book is about.
Give us some feedback about this book. What's on your heart?
Briefly talk about the genre; talk about who would, or would not, like the book.

interruptions at awkward times, and can allow you to foster a community where students feel that their questions are welcomed.

Conclusion

Literature can provide wonderful opportunities to analyze different aspects of life, characters, themes, writing competencies as expressed through the organization of text, the author's voice and word choice, and other writing traits that are employed for the purposes of having a specific impact on readers. However, we have found that the ability to analyze literature does not happen automatically. It takes practice with stopping to reflect on and connect to what is being read. These skills can be facilitated in the classroom through the use of the right tools. We hope that you will find the tools included in this chapter and in Chapter 3 to be helpful for the purposes of exploring and analyzing literature in deep and powerful ways.

5

Tools for Reading Informational Texts

We use highlighters and sticky notes. Every time I find something interesting, I highlight it and write my thoughts in the margins or on the sticky notes. It helps me internalize and process what I'm reading, and helps me understand the text better. —Gabriela, 8th grade

⚙ Exploring Text Features

When it comes to reading and comprehending informational texts, noticing and knowing how to use the text features is critically important. Text features include things like the following:

Organizational markers: titles, subtitles, headings, and subheadings

Enhanced text: bold print, colored print, italicized print, underlined print, and captions

Visually organized print: bulleted lists, numbered lists, indented text, text boxes, and sidebars

Graphic representations: photos, drawings and diagrams, graphs, charts, tables, figures, time lines, and maps

Reference features: table of contents, glossary, index, bibliography or list of references, and appendices

In narrative texts, authors often hold back information to provide suspense. Informational texts don't work this way. The purpose of the text can often be gleaned simply by reviewing text features that have been strategically placed throughout the text in order to support and enhance comprehension. You may find that many of your students have already figured out the benefits of noticing the text features before even delving into the text. In that case, you may only need to do minilessons with other, less strategic students who may need explicit help in noticing these features. Periodic conferencing can help you determine who needs help and who doesn't. Another good place to start with informational texts is to allow students to critically examine informational texts and discover, discuss, and critique the usefulness of the text features prior to explicitly teaching about them (see Figure 5.1). After students have discussed the text features, you can cover any that were missing within the sample texts. Continually revisiting and modeling the importance of using text features is an important component in helping students efficiently maneuver their ways around informational texts.

Figure 5.1

Sample Template for Exploring Text Features

Searching for Text Features

☐ Compare this text to the text in your independent reading book.

☐ Pay close attention to **anything** that is different. Make note of **anything** that is there to help you. For example, the color of the text, the look of the text, pictures, indented lists—anything that is different.

☐ What is placed there to help readers make sense of the text?

☐ How useful is it in helping you understand the text?

Page #	Describe it.	Why do you think that the author placed it there? How helpful is it?

⚙ Modeling Active and Zombie Reading

Eighth grade history teacher Liz Lubeskie's students readily admit that they struggle reading informational text. In order to support their learning in this area, Lubeskie brought in a textbook from her graduate class. She projected it on the board so that all of the students could see how she had actively marked up the text, and she allowed the students to ask her questions. Lubeskie recalls them asking questions like " 'What's all that writing in there?' 'Why are there different colors?' I told them that it was because I didn't understand it. I had to read it more than once." According to Lubeskie, this act of modeling how adults actively read text provides an important example of how the active reading behaviors that are being expected of students are still practiced in adulthood.

Active reading can also be modeled through role play. According to Potter, "I actually model with them the difference between what I call 'zombie reading' and 'active reading.' I'll ask them 'What does zombie reading look like?' And we will reenact it. We reenact active reading, too. Students demonstrate that they are constantly flipping the page, they have their pencils poised, they're scanning, they're marking up the text. For those who have fake-read since their own 4th grade slump, I think it really helps to just show them what active reading should look like".

⚙️ Marking Up the Text

Though this technique is used at the undergraduate college level, it holds potential for being used with younger students because it is explicit in illustrating what is expected from marked-up texts. Becoming fatigued with reading several hundred similar reading responses, coauthor William Himmele devised a new way to check for student understandings as students read through their assigned texts. Instead of requiring reading responses, which, because of their brevity, often only captured surface understandings, he instead started collecting students' actual texts in order to evaluate how each of the readers was making his or her way through the assigned readings. Without a doubt, it provided more freedom and better accountability as students were allowed to annotate the texts in their own ways. Figure 5.2 provides the directions and the rubric that was used to grade and provide feedback on the marked-up texts. Texts were initialed and dated at the beginning of the semester to ensure that each student was doing his or her own work as opposed to using or purchasing marked-up copies. If you present this technique, or a variation of it, to your elementary or secondary students, it may be motivating for them to know that several college professors are using this, too. These are the directions that were provided for the students:

Figure 5.2
Marked-up Text Rubric

The following scale is aimed at providing feedback on your marked-up text:

Highlighting, summaries, questions, elaborations, *and* connections in the margins of the text provided evidence that you actively interacted with the text.

1- Strongly Disagree   **2-Disagree**   **3-Somewhat**   **4-Agree**   **5-Strongly Agree**

Notations provided *evidence* of *deep* and *careful* reading, as well as *deep* and *careful* analysis of concepts.

1- Strongly Disagree   **2-Disagree**   **3-Somewhat**   **4-Agree**   **5-Strongly Agree**

The three-sentence summary captured the main points of the text. These main points were points that most readers would agree are significant enough to use as a wrap-up of the text.

1- Strongly Disagree   **2-Disagree**   **3-Somewhat**   **4-Agree**   **5-Strongly Agree**

The final "Aha's" provided evidence that you made thoughtful connections and deeply understood the significance of the concepts as they relate to your world and the world around you.

1- Strongly Disagree   **2-Disagree**   **3-Somewhat**   **4-Agree**   **5-Strongly Agree**

Directions for marking up your text:

1. As you read, interact with the text by highlighting, summarizing, questioning *and* commenting in the margins of your text. Your notations will be collected and graded.

   On the last page of each chapter, or at the end of each article, do the following:

2. Write a three-sentence summary that captures the main points of the chapter or article. These main points should be things on which most readers would agree are significant enough to use as a wrap-up of the chapter or article.

3. After your three-sentence summary, write an "Aha." What is the most significant thing that you read or an insight that you had as you read, and how does it relate to your world or to the world around you?

⚙ Independent Station Monitoring

While centers are commonplace in many elementary classrooms, they are less so in secondary classrooms. However, the need for minilessons and targeted instruction still exists for students in the secondary grades. Eighth grade teachers Liz Lubeskie and Matt Baker have incorporated centers into their classroom routines. In both of their classrooms, students shift through

20-minute intervals at independent work stations, collaborative work stations, and direct instruction stations where they work in small groups with the teacher. According to Lubeskie, "It's been like I was a new teacher again. It's completely different planning. Stations are something that are very common in an elementary classroom. But that's not typically the case in middle school classrooms. I've found that I love teaching with stations. The students notice that the class time goes so fast." For the directed teaching portion, Lubeskie and Baker may teach the same content three times or focus on minilessons that allow them to individualize the teaching. Lubeskie says, "I base it on what they are doing or on what they need. Sometimes, you're teaching the same thing three times, so it's exhausting, but the class time flies by." As an English teacher, Baker says that the benefits to stations are increased individualized instruction and increased comprehension and retention of content taught. According to Baker, "I can sit with students in more of a one-on-one setting to look at writing. I can also teach a targeted small-group lesson up there. It's more effective." Lubeskie uses the template in Figure 5.3 to keep track of progress at individual work stations.

Figure 5.3
Independent Station Monitoring Template

Name_____ Date _____

Today, I did the following:

Today, I was successful when . . .

Tomorrow, I hope to grow in the area of . . .

I can relate this work to my life because . . .

Used with permission from Liz Lubeskie and Brian Peters.

⚙ One-Word Summaries

Matt Baker will often finish off his lessons by asking students to create one-word summaries that capture the essence of that day's lesson. Baker's classroom is equipped with smooth desks. Because of this, the desks can also function as whiteboards. Baker asks student to use their "whiteboard desks" as a writing tablet for their one-word summaries and to provide a brief explanation as to why they chose that one word to capture the essence of the lesson. To debrief, have students one by one call out their one-word summary at the end of the activity. This functions as a Total Participation Technique in that it allows for a quick look at what all students learned. Total Participation Techniques will be reviewed in more depth in Chapter 6.

⚙ Concept Analogies

Analogies provide opportunities for looking at conceptual relationships from different angles. These concept analogies can be posted somewhere in the room for teachers to reference when they want students to describe their concept within the context of a certain relationship. For example, if the concept is *democracy*, a teacher might ask, "Metal is to shiny, as democracy is to _____." In order to complete the sentence, students have to think of an attribute of democracy. Using the desk as a whiteboard, this Total Participation Technique, as described above in the one-word summaries description, is a great way to get all students to quickly show you their thinking. Because the analogies may be somewhat confusing at first, teachers may want to allow students to do these in pairs until they have got the hang of them. Here are a few analogy frames that can be repeatedly used to explore relational concepts.

Opposite: Black is to white as *concept* is to _____.
Similarities: Big is to large as *concept* is to _____.
Causal: Clouds are to rain as *concept* is to _____.
Attribute: Metal is to shiny as *concept* is to _____.
Function: Key is to open as *concept* is to _____.
Dependence: Gas is to car as *concept* is to _____.
Sequence: Three is to four as *concept* is to _____.

⚙ Concept Mapping

Concept mapping is a wonderful technique for reviewing concepts in informational text and for exploring the connectedness of these concepts.

Developed by Novak and Gowin (1984), concept mapping allows students to physically manipulate concepts written on concept cards and articulate how the concepts are related to each other. Concept mapping has been typically studied in the field of science and has been shown to be an effective technique for increasing students' conceptual understandings (Güvenç & Ün Açikgöz, 2007; Kelly, 2007; Kinchin, 2000; Martin, 1994; Starr & Krajcik, 1990; Stice & Alvarez, 1987). Concept mapping is a great follow-up and wrap-up for difficult readings. It allows students to visually connect the concepts and go back to their readings in order to find the precise relationships between the concepts they are trying to describe. Concept mapping requires that students be able to not only understand that concepts are related, but also articulate the nature of the relationships between the concepts. A completed concept map should allow for a reader to read through the map without needing to leave the page to ask for clarification. Trust us on this one: Show the students a copy of a completed concept map, or use the example in Figure 5.5. Just telling students isn't enough. By showing them the depth you are expecting in your connections, you'll get better connections from them.

Teachers will need the following materials:

- A sample of a completed concept map (see Figure 5.5)
- 10–21 concept cards—Note: Too many concepts will confuse the students. (see Figure 5.4).
- A blank sheet of paper (to use as a mat)
- Glue (about one for every three students)
- Scissors (about one for every three students)

Step-by-Step Directions

Begin by reviewing the example of the completed concept map, pointing out several key features: (1) that you can read through the map without ever leaving the page; (2) that the connecting words and phrases help you understand what each of the concepts mean, or tell how they are related to each other.

1. **Cut and arrange.**
   Cut and lay out the cards in categories on top of the blank sheet of paper, or in a way that begins to tell how the concepts are related.

Figure 5.4
Hurricane Concept Cards

Hurricane	Inside the Eye	Storm Trackers
Spinning Winds	Over the Sea	Lightning
Power	Eye Wall	Feeder Bands
Measuring the Storm's Strength	Storm Surge	Wind Gusts
Tropical Depressions	Tropical Storm	Fuel for Hurricanes
Naming a Hurricane	The Most Important Thing About a Hurricane	

2. **Share and finalize.**
   Share your concept map with one other person. Make any final changes to your concept map.
3. **Glue.**
   Glue down your concept cards.
4. **Add connector words and phrases.**
   Start connecting your concepts using clear language that demonstrates your understanding of the concepts and how they are related.

Figure 5.5

Caleb's Concept Map

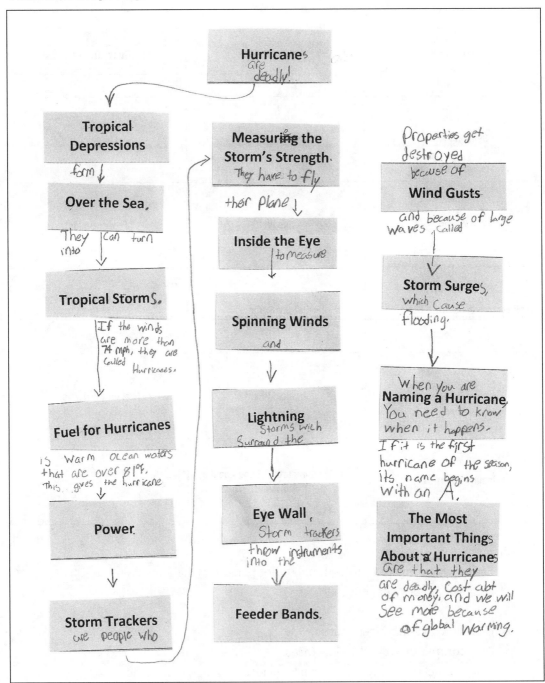

⚙ Content-Based *I Am* Poems

I Am poems have been circulating around schools since at least the 1970s. They are typically used for students in "getting to know you" activities. Content-based *I Am* poems take the same frames and add a twist in that they rely on students' understanding of the content that has been taught. They can be done from the perspective of a person (see Figure 5.6) or from the perspective of a concept (See Figure 5.7). It's easy for students to write these poems using non-content-related themes. In order to ensure that students include content-specific themes, give them a concept bank to reference.

These poems work well in almost any content area. Seventh and 8th grade history and science teachers Jacqueline Neudorf and Rolwand Hayward asked their students to create *I Am* poems on the topics of ancient Greece and viscosity. The ancient Greece poems put students in the place of Spartan and Athenian families, making mention of the realities of ancient Greece within the historical timeframe being studied. The viscosity poems had titles like "I Am High-Viscocity Molasses" and "I Am Low-Viscosity Apple Juice." Concepts such as flow rates, buoyancy, and mass were included to demonstrate an understanding of the content taught.

Step-by-Step Directions

1. **Create a concept bank.**
   Create a list of about five to eight concepts that should be clearly and logically articulated in student *I Am* poems. Or create a longer list, and ask students to select a certain number from within that list.

2. **Fill in the *I Am* poem frame.**
   Ask students to fill in the *I Am* poem frame from the perspective of the concept or person being written about, including their concepts from the concept bank.

   I am
   I wonder
   I hear
   I see
   I want
   I am

Figure 5.6

I Am Poem Based on a Person

I Am Poem using a person as the topic:

For the *I Am* poem about Thaddeus Stevens, students were given these directions:
Your *I Am* Poem should make clear and logical references to each of the following:

The 13th Amendment
The 14th Amendment
His occupation
His personal beliefs
His relationships
His relationship with Andrew Johnson

I am Thaddeus Stevens

I am Thaddeus Stevens.
I wonder if the 14th Amendment will be enough.
I hear the sound of my wife rejoicing over the success of the 13th
    Amendment.
I see African Americans beaten and working hard, I become their lawyer for
    free.
I want my tombstone to state something about how all people are equal.
I am Thaddeus Stevens.

I pretend Andrew Johnson has been impeached.
I feel that there should be no slavery, and that all African Americans should
    have the same rights, too.
I touch the lives of many.
I worry that the 14th Amendment will never be passed.
I cry when people argue with me about the rights of African Americans.
I am Thaddeus Stevens.

I understand how important these Amendments are.
I say, "Equality of man before his Creator."
I dream that one day everyone will treat each other with respect.
I try to write the 14th Amendment so that African Americans will have legal
    rights.
I hope that one day African Americans will also be allowed to vote.
I am Thaddeus Stevens.

                                        By Sneha and Gabriela, 8th Grade

Figure 5.7

I *Am* Poem Based on a Concept

I *Am* poem using a concept or an inanimate object as the topic:

For the *I Am* poem about the Thirteenth Amendment, students were given these directions:

Your *I Am* Poem should make clear and logical references to at least 5 of the following:

    The 14th Amendment
    The 15th Amendment
    Thaddeus Stevens
    Abraham Lincoln
    The Civil War
    Abolitionist
    Slavery
    The North
    The South

I Am the Thirteenth Amendment

I am the Thirteenth Amendment.
I wonder if slavery is going to be abolished.
I see the Civil War going on and Abraham Lincoln behind the North's army.
I want slaves to be freed.
I am the Thirteenth Amendment.

I pretend that the 14th Amendment doesn't need to be made.
I feel that we need more amendments because I don't have enough
    statements to protect people.
I touch the sound waves of arguments going on around me.
I worry about not getting passed.
I cry from my worry.
I am the Thirteenth Amendment.

I understand the feelings of Thaddeus Stevens.
I say positive words about myself.
I dream that no slaves would be property.
I try to keep myself from negative statements.
I hope that slaves will be free.
I am the Thirteenth Amendment.

By Guarav, 5th Grade

I pretend
I feel
I touch
I worry
I cry
I am

I understand
I say
I dream
I try
I hope
I am

⚙ Found Poems

A found poem is a low-risk activity that asks students to find critical words within a text that are important for deeply understanding the reading. There are many variations to this activity. Liz Lubeskie and Matt Baker asked students to individually read a passage and highlight what spoke to them. Lubeskie explains, "I told them to think about what really stood out. For example, if they read it and thought, 'Wow, that meant something,' then they were asked to highlight it." Lubeskie asked students to work in pairs. Students were asked to share their highlighted portions with their partners. Lubeskie noted, "A lot of them were finding the same things highlighted. So, those were automatically going to be in their found poems. And then they talked about what each of them had highlighted and they debated why each was most important. 'Where do you think we should put it?' and they started formulating stanzas."

Matt Baker took the same idea and focused on the introduction to a book on emigration. He noted that while each of the students was successful in including the main ideas, the found poems were all unique. "It was interesting. Some students did it from the more hopeful standpoint, and other students looked at it from the angle of all of the struggles that people went through. So they did it on the same introduction, but it is interesting how they were all so personal and different." Baker also noted that while writing poetry might not have been a favorite activity for some of the students, "the found poems are creative and nobody complains." Lubeskie agrees: "There is such great energy when the students compare what they highlighted. You'll hear 'Oooh, ooooh I have that highlighted, too.' " A completed found poem is included in Figure 5.8.

Figure 5.8

Tyler and Rachael's Found Poem

"The Verdict"

The charge
Tax Evasion
Arrest has nothing to do with taxes
This is to put an end to his work
A felony

Judge is white
Prosecuting attorney
Also white
Twelve jurors
All white

George Wallace
"Segregation now, segregation tomorrow, segregation forever"
Unjust laws
"Fill up the jails!"

Sit-ins
Woolworth store
Non-violent protest
Democracy and segregation
Cannot exist together

999 pieces of evidence
No evidence of fraud
All white jury
NOT GUILTY.

By Tyler and Rachael, 8th Grader

Step-by-Step Directions

1. **Read.**
   Ask students to read through a particular passage of text.
2. **Review and select key words or phrases.**
   Ask students to reread the passage, identifying 50 words or a specific number of lines (Matt Baker asked for 10–12 lines) that carry significant weight or represent the most valuable ideas in that passage.

(Note: For longer passages, choose more words. The student sample in Figure 5.8 contains 75 words.) If you have photocopies, ask students to highlight the words; if you are working straight from the text, ask students to simply copy their words onto a separate sheet of paper.

3. **Rearrange and finalize.**

Rearrange the words so that the main message of the passage is clearly conveyed.

⚙ Inferencing with Younger Students

Carmen Rowe works with English language learners in K–5 settings. Though her students are learning English, she makes it a goal to present grade-level standards in scaffolded ways so students can be successful. For teaching inferencing with 3rd graders, Rowe brought in her husband's backpack, which contained several novels, a large pair of soccer shoes, exercise equipment, and other random items. Carmen began her lesson by explaining that someone had left their backpack in her office and the students needed to help her figure out to whom it belonged. As she pulled out each item, students began making inferences. The person was obviously a strong reader, because the books contained several hundred pages. The person was obviously an adult, because no student at their school would be able to fit into the soccer shoes. Carmen peppered her explanations with variations of the term *infer*. For example, "Oh, so you are inferring that this person is an adult. That's a good inference." She began recording their inferences on a piece of chart paper, finally explaining that the backpack belonged to her husband and that they had just learned how to make inferences. She then began modeling for them how to make text-based inferences. The chart remains in the room, so that she can reference it whenever she asks the students to infer. Rowe will say, "Do you remember when we made inferences about the backpack? What kinds of inferences can we make about what the character is feeling?"

⚙ Family Metaphors Template

In preparation for more sophisticated uses of the concept of metaphors, Rowe also taught her English language learners about the meanings of metaphors by using something with which they could relate. Rowe began by reading a poem about her family that compared her family to a tree, with each family member representing a different part of the tree. After modeling how to create a metaphor poem, she guided them through their own family metaphor poem (Figure 5.9). Students were successful in creating beautiful metaphorical poetry because they started with something with which they were familiar. As Rowe's current students become more grounded in their uses of symbolism and metaphors, the ideas will be used and applied to more abstract concepts that they will be taught.

Figure 5.9

Template for Family Metaphor Poem

Writing a Metaphor Poem About Your Family

Directions:

1. Determine the BIG overall metaphor for your poem (for example: My family is a tree). Write the BIG overall metaphor for your family below.
2. List the members of your family in the first column.
3. In the second column, labeled Traits/Description, describe each family member.
4. In the third column, labeled Comparison, compare each family member to something, without using like or as (for example: My father is the trunk).
5. On a separate sheet of paper put each comparison into a sentence supporting your metaphor with details. Be sure to include a title for your poem and to state the BIG overall metaphor for your family.

Overall Metaphor:

Family Member	Traits/ Description	Comparison

By Carmen Rowe; used with permission.

Creating Headings or Subheadings

Earlier, we talked about the uses of multiple sources and primary sources to bring multiple perspectives to the teaching of complex issues and concepts. On the one hand, the Internet provides easy access to what was once a very inconvenient task of compiling sources through paper copies of texts. On the other hand, these texts are typically not student-friendly. English teacher Matt Baker saw that as an opportunity, rather than an obstacle. For one text that included minimal uses of headings, he asked students to create the headings for each of the sections. Much like his one-word summaries activity, students had to identify the purposes for the various paragraphs and decide which ones went together, what headings to assign, and how to meaningfully do that using as few words as possible. They also had be able to justify their headings. Baker was persistent in making students explain unclear headings in the margins. He says, "I wouldn't let them come up with random titles. They had to provide a rationale for why. As they read, I wanted them to analyze, 'How is this text actually structured?'" As teachers begin to take advantage of easy access to multiple perspectives on content-area topics, asking the students to create headings and subheadings is a wonderful way to help students organize their thinking about the text.

"Teach Me" Lessons

Eighth grade history teacher Liz Lubeskie has students create a unit that she calls "Teach Me" lessons. Students actually prepare a history presentation on a given topic and, using any electronic or digital means, present their "Teach Me" lessons to the class. There are several components that make this lesson memorable. Lubeskie requires that students dress professionally for their presentation. Like any teacher, they are referred to as Mr. ___ or Miss ___. They begin their lesson with an essential question, and they provide a handout on which their classmates can take notes. Some of the students make use of some of the interactive techniques that are a staple in Lubeskie's classroom. Lubeskie shared, "One student put up his essential question and asked them to talk about it with their shoulder partners. He wore a tie and looked very professional." Note: Essential questions refer to broad questions that are "not answerable with finality—in a brief sentence . . . . Their aim is to stimulate thought, to provoke inquiry, and to spark more questions" (Wiggins & McTighe, 2005, p. 106).

The "Teach Me" lessons are graded on the quality of the content; aspects related to the presentation, such as the presenter's ability to engage the audience; and the quality of required components, such as the essential question and the quiz. For example, with regard to the presenter's ability to engage the audience, one aspect that Lubeskie looks at is eye contact and whether the presenter faced the slides or the audience. Here is the general format for the content that is required by Lubeskie in the "Teach Me" lessons:

Slide 1: Title Slide
Slide 2: Essential Question Slide
Slides 3–7: Informational Slides (minimum of 5)
Summary Slide: Answer the Essential Question
Quiz Slide: 5 Student-Friendly Questions. These may take up two slides.
Quiz Answers
References and Bibliography Slide

One of the things that makes the "Teach Me" lessons function well is the modeling of what a good presentation looks like and what a weak presentation looks like. Both Liz Lubeskie and Matt Baker model how not to do a presentation, by cramming words onto a slide and reading the slide to the class. They ask students to analyze what went wrong. According to Lubeskie, "Students will say things like 'Why were you looking at the slide?' or 'I couldn't hear you.' I tell them, 'Remember, don't insult your students' intelligence by reading them a slide. They can read. You give them the details; you spice it up' " Students are allowed to bring index cards, but there is an emphasis on eye contact and on engaging their audience.

In order to combat students' tendencies to read from the slides, Baker does not allow students to put anything more than a title and a picture on each slide. According to Baker, "Their slide can say 'Causes', and then they can talk about the causes of the problem, and the slide is allowed to have pictures, and that's it."

For Lubeskie's lessons, students are also required to include a five-question quiz. According to Lubeskie, "This is harder than it looks. Students need to really understand their topic to pick their five points; plus it keeps the class on their toes while the teacher is presenting." To cap off the unit, the students use peer presentations as resources for writing an essay in response to an overall unit prompt. According to Lubeskie, "They have to take notes while their friends are presenting. Their essay question is very simple: 'How did the United States change from 1800 to 1850?' They need to include a minimum of three resources. The resources need to be their peers' presentations. They need to cite with details, and explain. For example, they'd say, 'In Mr. Brookhart's presentation, he discussed . . . .'"

Conclusion

For the vast majority of students we interviewed and conferenced with, it is clear that the greatest challenges they experience involve making sense of informational texts. This chapter focuses on providing teachers with tools for helping students learn to independently and critically read informational texts. Several of the tools and techniques make use of text-based student interaction to create environments that support students as they articulate what they know and help them learn from each other. Regardless of the standards-focused increased rigor in skills and abilities that may be expected from students, increased rigor will not erase the need for well-planned scaffolding. In fact, increased rigor only increases the need for scaffolds. These tools can help teachers provide students the needed scaffolds for engaging with challenging texts and provide teachers with evidence that students have processed the content using higher-order thinking.

6

Total Participation Techniques and Tools for Framing Text-Based Peer Interactions

Hearing others share helps me learn more. Like when Caleb and Mackenzie shared their reading techniques. I can use those.
—Michala, 7th grade

Total Participation Techniques

Picture that student who is always raising his hand to answer your questions. He's constantly "on." He's focused, he's processing, and he's making connections. He's getting quite an education, isn't he? What about the other students, the ones who never raise their hands and look as though they are a million miles away? What kind of an education are they getting? Throughout this book, we've addressed the importance of higher-order thinking. We'd like to briefly address the importance of making these higher-order thinking opportunities available to all of the students in your class, rather than just a select few. Recall the list of questions aimed at analyzing literature and informational texts (Figures 3.2 and 3.3). Well, those analytical questions will do very little good to the majority of your class if you let a few students monopolize the conversation. Quick-writes (brief written responses to prompts) are a great solution to this. One 8th grade student whom we interviewed admitted to being that student who is a million miles away. According to this student, "I drift off a lot. Like, one of the classes I go to I call 'my daydreaming class.' When I go in there, I daydream. But in Ms. Keely's class you can't daydream, because if you do, you're gonna miss something important, and at the end of class she asks you to write about what we went over in class, so if you were daydreaming, she'll know you weren't paying attention. So that helps."

Total Participation Techniques (Himmele & Himmele, 2009, 2011) are a solution to the daydreaming in class. They are techniques that can help you get more bang for your teaching buck because they provide you with evidence of active participation and higher-order thinking from all of your students at the same time. Several of the teaching tools in this book function as Total Participation Techniques (TPTs) because they allow you to engage all students at the same time using higher-order thinking. All of the tools in this chapter function as TPTs. When students are all participating in activities that require higher-order thinking collectively, students end up enlightening each other.

Remember to Ripple

We believe that one of the most important concepts that we discuss in our books are the concepts of the beach ball (2011) and the ripple (2009, 2011). The beach ball represents the question. With the beach ball scenario, the teacher asks a question in a traditional Q & A format (the teacher tosses the beach ball to a student). One student responds (he catches the beach ball and tosses it back). This happens for a few rounds, while the majority of the class sits passively listening to a few students as they carry on an animated conversation with the teacher. It probably happens in the "daydreaming class" described earlier. We all can fall into the trap of getting caught up in a conversation with the most animated students, while the rest of the class is let off the hook. In contrast to the beach ball, the ripple is in the shape of concentric circles. The inner circle is that higher-order question that is now posed to each student. Every student is required to individually respond to it in the form of an informal quick-write or via another TPT. The inner circle is followed up by the middle circle, where each student pairs up with another or works in a smaller group to share their answers. The middle circle is followed by the outer circle, which represents the questions posed to the whole class. In other words, when posing higher-order questions, we should begin by giving each individual student an opportunity to respond. Once students have had a chance to think individually and then share their response with a peer, they are more ready to share their responses with the class as a whole. Your discussions will be more lively, and you will have evidence from each student that he or she spent time processing your higher-order prompt. It's a very simple concept that we would love to see catch on, for the sake of the students.

Using the ripple, higher-order prompts are processed in this order:

1. Individual Students (All students individually respond to the prompts.)

2. Pairs or Small Groups (All students share in pairs or small groups.)

3. Whole Group (Volunteers share, or pairs or small groups call out a sentence summary when they are called on.)

According to high school English teacher Susan Grammer, "The concept of the ripple seems to have occupied a permanent place in the forefront of my mind. The idea of having students first work alone, then with a partner, and then with a larger group is nothing grand. However, when a colleague and I were preparing our TPT in-service, we found ourselves deviating from this paradigm and moving to a beach ball paradigm. We had to force ourselves to be intentional in our approach because time after time, we—seasoned teachers—found ourselves guilty of planning a few rounds of beach ball. Now, I am better at recognizing my beach ball habits and substituting the ripple instead."

ELL teacher Carmen Rowe talks about the effects of the beach ball approach in linguistically diverse classrooms. "I have observed classes in which partner and small-group work was going on, yet upon closer inspection it was evident that the ELLs were marginalized. Native English speakers and fast processors often hijack conversations unless the teacher is alert to it. That independent reflection time is so important for ELLs. They need time to process the content. Quick-writes are essential. The quick-writes could be jotting down lingering questions about the text, a statement that resonated with the student, or a quick response to a teacher-directed prompt. Without it, you can't be sure that everyone is processing." Higher-order thinking takes time. Processing at deep analytical levels requires more time for some students than for others. If you play beach ball with your higher-order questions, for most of the students, you're wasting really good questions that might otherwise be put to good use.

This chapter contains Total Participation Techniques that foster interactions based on what students are reading. For additional techniques, refer to our 2011 text, *Total Participation Techniques: Making Every Student an Active Learner.*

Framing Student Interactions

So much of the quality of your lessons will be dependent on your ability to effectively foster positive student-to-student interactions. After all, expecting that students take risks by attempting higher-order processing in front of their peers requires that you establish a safe and accepting environment. Some teachers do this implicitly. For the rest of us, it takes practice. For example, when we asked 7th grader Jaycie what exactly helped her become a more avid reader that year, we didn't expect her response. Rather than focus on teaching techniques, she started by describing the safe, accepting climate in the classroom that allowed her and her classmates to delve deeply into the process of reading and writing and the risk taking that it entails. According to Jaycie, this safe environment "changed the way that we talk to each other. A lot of the way she taught included our body language and how we treat each other. We would sit in a circle where we could all see each other. When anybody was speaking we all had to make eye contact. It got to where people were getting more and more comfortable about sharing their feelings. And when people would give me eye contact, I felt safer and was able to share my feelings. That helped a lot." Before expecting students to take risks, we will need to establish procedures that ensure that all students feel safe to participate.

Building a classroom community is essential if we want students to be willing to open up and share. It's also essential because the collective voices add to the tapestry of learning. Ninth grader Alison stated it beautifully when she said, "Interaction is a must when reading and writing. Not everyone sees things the same way or has been through the same experiences. In fact, no one has. So because no two people have the exact same train of thought, some people see things that others miss. Some people find significance in things that others don't. Interaction helps everyone to understand books in a very different way." There is strength in the diversity of thought, and our students miss out when they don't listen to each other's perspectives. The Art of Conversation is an experiential simulation to help students understand first-hand the positive results that good listening skills have on speakers, and the negative results that poor listening skills have on speakers. It is best conducted early in the school year to help you establish expectations with regard to listening behaviors that foster a community of inquiry.

⚙ The Art of Conversation Simulation

In this simulation, students will be given roles of speakers and specific types of listeners. This activity requires a well-intentioned misleading of the students who will be playing the speaker roles. Group members will be made up of students playing the following roles: *The Speaker, The Good Listener, The Multitasker,* and *The Easily Distracted.* Teachers will need photocopies of a different role card for each group member (Figure 6.1). As we stated earlier, we highly recommend doing this activity early in the year to help set some expectations for group discussions.

Step-by-Step Directions

1. **Create groups of four.**

   Split your class into groups of four. For smaller or larger groups, duplicate or eliminate roles, making sure that every group has at least one Speaker and one Good Listener role.

2. **Select the speakers.**

   Select a speaker, or ask for one volunteer who is not afraid to talk, from each group and give them the description of the Speaker role (see Figure 6.1).

3. **Distribute listener roles.**

   The roles for each listener should be kept a secret from the speakers. Tell the class that the papers contain things to keep in mind as they actively listen. Hand out a different role card to each person in each of the groups.

4. **Role-play the simulation.**

   During the simulation, circulate around the room. The Multitaskers will need for you to circulate around the room in order to fulfill their roles.

5. **Debrief.**

   After an appropriate time (about five minutes), share the real purpose of the activity. Tell the students to share their roles with the speaker and tell them to discuss insights with their small group using the debriefing questions. After small groups have had an opportunity to share and debrief, ask volunteers to share their group's insights in a whole-group format. Record insights to refer to when discussing active listening habits.

Variation

There is also value in conducting this activity in a "fishbowl" format, where four participants conduct the simulation while the class observes and takes notes. Though it has the disadvantage of not allowing everyone to feel the experience of being heard or ignored, it does allow them to carefully observe and record each of the participants' reactions, and it can also be easier to manage.

Figure 6.1

The Art of Conversation Simulation

Speaker Role: Select from one of the three topics below (a sport, a book , or a video game). Your job is to respond to the questions for the topic you have selected. You will be allowed to refer to these questions as you speak, but try not to focus so much on this sheet of paper. Instead, try to focus on your group members.

Topic: A Favorite Sport

1. Tell about your favorite sport.
2. Explain why it is your favorite sport.
3. Talk about your personal experiences with this sport.
4. Explain how this sport is played.
5. Explain what it takes to be a good player of this sport.
6. Explain how you developed an interest in this sport.
7. Talk about other sports that you also find interesting.

Topic: A Favorite Book

1. Tell about your favorite book.
2. Explain why it is your favorite book.
3. Talk about what happens or what is written in the book.
4. Tell about your favorite part.
5. Talk about who would like this book and tell why.
6. Talk about other books that you also found interesting.

Topic: A Video Game

1. Tell about your favorite video game.
2. Explain why it is your favorite game.
3. Talk about your personal experiences with this game.
4. Explain how the game is played.
5. Explain what it takes to be a good player of this game.
6. Explain how you developed an interest in the game.
7. Talk about other games that you also find interesting.

The Good Listener Role

Shhhhh. Keep your role a secret. You will be playing the role of the good listener. As the speaker is talking, *face your body toward the speaker,* keep your *eyes on the speaker,* and nod to demonstrate that you are following along. Try not to laugh.

Remember that we are trying to simulate how real people act in a conversation. Try to keep your actions natural, and don't exaggerate. In other words, don't nod excessively like a bobble-head toy, but do nod. And don't overdo the eye contact with a creepy awkward stare. It's OK to look down for a half-second, but do it so that it looks like your still thinking about what the speaker is saying.

The Easily Distracted Role

Shhhhhh. Keep your role a secret. You will be playing the role of the student who is easily distracted. When the speaker is speaking, *be listening for about 10 seconds,* then *stop, break eye contact,* and *look around for about three seconds* at the other groups or at the clock. Repeat this behavior about four times and then try to go ahead and listen for the rest of the speaker's presentation. Try not to laugh.

Remember that we are trying to simulate how real people act in a conversation. Don't make it obvious that you are counting or that you are deliberately looking away.

The Multitasker Role

Shhhhhh. Keep your role a secret. You will be playing the role of the multitasker. Multitasking is when people try to do more than one thing at a time. You will *pretend to be distracted by needing to reread this paper.* When the speaker begins talking, listen to the conversation for about five seconds. Then check to see if the teacher is looking. *As soon as the teacher is not looking, start carefully rereading this paper.* When you notice that the teacher is nearby or is looking, start paying attention to the speaker. *Repeat this for four or five times,* then go ahead and try to listen to the rest of the speaker's presentation.

Remember that we are trying to simulate how real people act in a conversation. While it should look like you're trying to get away with something, try not to exaggerate your actions or let the speaker know that it is an act. Try not to laugh.

Debriefing the Art of Conversation Simulation

1. Speaker, share about what you noticed and how you felt.
2. Listeners, share what you noticed about the speaker's behaviors.
   At whom did the speaker look during most of the conversation? Why?
   To whom did the speaker talk?
   When you started being a better listener, did the speaker's behaviors change?
3. What connections do you see with regard to this activity and real life?
4. Brainstorm behaviors that describe good listening skills and behaviors that describe poor listening skills. Talk about not only what the behaviors look like, but the results in terms of how the behaviors make people feel.
5. As a group, sum up your discussion by creating a list of your top three to five guidelines for demonstrating good listening skills.

⚙ Bounce Cards

Teaching students how to actively listen to each other may be the easier part of the art of conversation. When it comes to helping them contribute and share, you will find that many do not have the words. Bounce Cards (Himmele & Himmele, 2011) provide an avenue for students to share using three main tasks:

1. To bounce something off of what their peers said

2. To sum up what their peers said

3. To ask questions regarding what their peers said

Bounce Cards provide the sentence starters for these three tasks. According to Keely Potter, "The Bounce Cards have been huge, and for students who are not used to talking to each other, they were absolutely critical. It gave them the words to say. They have been absolutely critical. Now it is so engrained, they'll say, 'I'm hearing you say that . . . but I have a different way of looking at it . . . .' I don't even have to cue them anymore—it's automatic." Once Potter's students got the gist of what the Bounce Cards were asking them to do, they started adding their own personal touches and phrases to the Bounce Cards. We encourage you to create a poster or chart that includes these sentence starters, and also to provide copies for students to use as bookmarks. As the students develop their own phrases, they can add them to their bookmarks or they can be added to the class chart. Before you introduce the Bounce Cards (see Figure 6.2) or a Bounce Card chart, select a student to help you model their use with good and stagnant conversations. Bounce Cards facilitate the use of discussion-based Total Participation Techniques.

Bounce Cards with Blogs and Peer Posts

We have also found that Bounce Cards provide an important scaffold for students who are electronically responding to peers' posts in the form of blogs. The prompts help students gracefully post an objection without getting personal. If you blog with your students or if you ask them to reply to prompts or posts, giving each student a Bounce Card can support them by helping them read prompts and posts from different angles and know where to begin, in terms of responding.

Figure 6.2
Bounce Cards

> **Bounce:**
> Take what your classmate(s) said and bounce an idea off of it. For example, you can start your sentences with
>> "That reminds me of…"
>> "I agree, because…"
>> "True, another example is when…"
>> "That's a great point…"
>
> **Sum it up:**
> Rephrase what was said in a shorter version. For example, you can start your sentences with
>> "I hear you saying that…"
>> "So, if I understand you correctly…"
>> "I like how you said…"
>
> **Ask questions:**
> Understand what your classmates mean by asking them questions. For example, you can start your questions with
>> "Can you tell me more about that?"
>> "I'm not sure I understand…"
>> "I see your point, but what about…?"
>> "Have you thought about…?"

Pérsida and William Himmele, 2011, *Total Participation Techniques*, p. 69.

Discussion-Based Total Participation Techniques

 Music Mingle

For a simple way to pair students, Liz Lubeskie uses an activity she calls Music Mingle. This Total Participation Technique, similar to the game musical chairs, asks students to walk around the room while music is playing. When the music stops, students are asked to turn to the nearest person. That person will be their partner for the activity. In order to ensure that this activity flows smoothly, Lubeskie asks students to adhere to the following rules:

1. No turning away from someone when the music stops.

2. Be respectful of people's opinions and answers.

3. No stopping and talking to the same person more than once.

4. No side chatter is allowed—only prompt-based conversations are permitted.

⚙ Bell Networking

Bell Networking is another simple way of pairing students. Students are given several prompts to respond to—first individually via quick-writes, then in random pairs. Students begin by finding anyone who does not sit at their table or with whom they haven't spoken that day. During this Total Participation Technique, the students discuss their responses to the first prompt. At the sound of a bell, students are asked to wrap up their thoughts and find another person with whom they should begin discussing their responses to the next prompt. Interesting bell sounds can be easily accessed on YouTube. Instead of a handheld bell, we'll often click "play" on the video to signal when students should stop and move on to a new partner and a new prompt. Bell Networking adds a touch of spice, interaction, and movement to a typical time of debriefing. For best results, use rules 2 through 4 described for Music Mingle.

⚙ The Picture Walk

The Picture Walk is a powerful Total Participation Technique activity that allows students to analyze pictures from their informational texts prior to reviewing and reading their texts (Himmele & Himmele, 2009). It is a fun activity because students work in small groups traveling from picture to picture analyzing aspects of the pictures. The power in this activity is dependent on the prompts. Use higher-order prompts that prepare students for what they will be reading or that pique curiosity regarding what they will be reading. Students respond to the prompts by writing on Post-its and attaching them near each picture. We typically use two prompts per picture, or one or two prompts that apply to all of the pictures.

Teachers will need the following materials:

- Six or seven pictures from the selected text posted and spaced out evenly around the room

- A bell or other form of alerting students
- Sticky notes for student comments

Step-by-Step Directions

1. **Select and post pictures.**
   Select six or seven of the text's pictures to enlarge, print, and post around the room, evenly spaced. Use enough pictures so that students can work in small groups of about four.

2. **Students respond to prompts.**
   Ask small groups to stand at a specific picture, so that each picture has only one small group analyzing it. Post the prompts where everyone can see them and ask students to discuss the prompts, and record their responses on Post-its (either individually or as a group). If each picture has its own separate prompt, post the individual prompts near each corresponding picture.

3. **Students move to next picture and repeat.**
   After most of the students appear to have finished responding to the prompt, ring a bell to notify students that it is time for them to wrap up their analysis and move clockwise or counterclockwise to the next picture.

⚙ The Likert Scale

The Likert scale allows for students to select a position on a topic, draft a rationale to their position, discuss their positions with like-minded classmates, and record rationales for the other four positions. This Total Participation Technique is an excellent activity for focusing on themes and concepts within texts that present the options for multiple positions. Be sure to steer clear of highly controversial topics, which may result in students feeling alienated. To begin, teachers should post these five signs around the room: Strongly Agree, Agree, Undecided, Disagree, and Strongly Disagree, and present their text-based prompt to the students.

Step-by-Step Directions

1. **Select a position and write a rationale.**
   Using the scale, students are asked to take a position on a certain text-based prompt. Students record the prompt on their template (see

Figure 6.3). Students select one of the five positions and write down their rationale under that designated spot in their template.

2. **Students stand at designated spots and discuss.**

   Students should go to the area in the room where their position is posted. For example, all the students who selected "Strongly Agree," should stand near the sign that says "Strongly Agree." Students should each discuss what they wrote as their rationales. Teachers can divide large groups into smaller groups of about five or six students.

3. **Write summary statement.**

   After discussing rationales, each group should prepare summary statements that sum up what they discussed. It should include all of the rationales (with like rationales grouped into one statement).

4. **Record peers' rationales.**

   Each group should then present their rationales to the class. Groups that are listening should be summarizing and recording their peers' rationales on the designated spots on their templates. By the end of the activity, all students should have something written in all of the areas of the template that were covered.

Figure 6.3

Likert Scale Template

	Responses & Rationales		
Quick-Write & Groups' Rationales	Today's prompt is:		
SA **Strongly Agree**			
A **Agree**			
U **Undecided** **(with rationale)**			
D **Disagree**			
SD **Strongly Disagree**			

⚙ Four Corners

This Total Participation Technique is an interactive activity that allows students to select one of four teacher-selected text excerpts to discuss with their peers. To begin, teachers should post the letters A, B, C, and D, evenly spaced throughout the room. Teachers will need four excerpts from the text that students will be discussing. For example, the following statements are from Stephen Krashen's book *The Power of Reading* (2004).

A: "Those who say they read more, read and write better" (p. 8).

B: "Spelling instruction, when it works, may only succeed in helping children learn to spell words that they would have learned to spell on their own anyway" (p. 27).

C: "There is considerable evidence that comic books can and do lead to more 'serious' reading" (p. 97).

D: "Rewarding reading sends a message that reading is unpleasant or not worth doing without a reward" (p. 117).

Step-by-Step Directions

1. **Select an excerpt and write a rationale.**

   Students select an excerpt on which to prepare a quick-write. Their writing does not have to agree with the statement they selected. They can elaborate on it, question it, or agree or disagree with it (use template in Figure 6.4).

2. **Students stand at designated spots and discuss.**

   Students should go to the area in the room where their position is posted. For example, all the students who selected A should stand near the sign that says A. Students should each discuss their quick-writes. Teachers can divide large groups into smaller groups of about five or six students.

3. **Write summary statement.**

   After discussing quick-writes, each group should prepare statements that summarize what they discussed. It should include major themes from the various quick-writes (with like themes grouped into one statement).

4. **Record peers' summaries.**

   Each group should then present their summaries to the class. Groups that are listening should be summarizing and recording their peers' summaries on the designated spots on their templates.

Figure 6.4

Four Corners Template

	Responses & Rationales
Quick-Write & Groups' Discussion Summaries	Quick summary of the prompt I chose:
A	
B	
C	
D	

Conclusion

In this chapter, we introduced the concepts of rippling higher-order prompts as a way of engaging all students in the content. We also introduced various Total Participation Techniques for helping students become engaged with texts. TPTs provide a structure for ensuring that all of your students are participating using higher-order thinking. They are easy to implement and can really add spice to an otherwise dull lesson. Most important, TPTs are great for providing teachers with tangible evidence that students are cognitively engaged with what they've read and the content being taught.

7

A Tool for Teaching Students How to Respond to Constructed Response Prompts

Using the same framework districtwide or even schoolwide allows students to see that the citation of text and an explanation of the relationship of the citation to the prompt is a universal skill that is needed in all classes.
—Michelle Trasborg, K–12 Communications and ESL Supervisor

We would love to say that all writing can be authentic, based on interest, relevance, and a desire to celebrate words. However, we know of excellent student writers who can effectively paint pictures with words and create emotionally stirring narratives, yet freeze up when faced with a constructed response essay prompt that they find has no relevance to their lives. Those same students are the ones who often preoccupy themselves with adding beautiful imagery or hold back a surprise ending that defeats the purpose of writing an informational piece. We know of other students who thrive on structure and linear approaches to attacking a problem. For these students, it is helpful to have a plan of attack with regard to text-based constructed response prompts. In this chapter, we will present a writing formula that is being used successfully at Conestoga Valley School District in Lancaster, Pennsylvania.

When it comes to answering constructed response prompts, "text-based evidence" has become the hot new phrase for content-area teachers and language arts teachers alike. Although it would appear as though gathering text-based evidence is a simple enough expectation for young writers, several challenges emerge that make this expectation more complicated than it would seem. A critical and common problem area for students is the ability to write a targeted response that addresses the actual question. In many cases, students are so often asked to look for relevance in text that relevance becomes the main point of everything they want to write, even if the prompt is asking them to address a differing perspective. Combatting this tendency requires explicit instruction around how to know what the prompt is asking and how to go about finding the evidence that is needed to answer it.

Additional challenges stem from helping students develop a game plan for writing and not becoming overwhelmed when they read a prompt that asks them to do several things at once. Curricular leader Michelle Trasborg finds that this is especially challenging when it comes to struggling readers, ELLs, and student with special needs. According to Trasborg, "They are often overwhelmed by the task of answering open-ended questions. They need simple steps to follow that will help them break down the task and give them clear direction."

Once students understand that an expectation is that they include evidence from the text, how students organize and expand on this text-based evidence is what often makes the difference between a coherent piece that flows and one that creates gaps between the students' intentions in embedding what they feel is appropriate evidence to answer a question and their ability to clearly articulate why certain citations are included in their writings. According to 8th grade teacher Matt Baker, "When students are asked to do research, the first thing they want to do is to just throw out quotes. It's easy for them to simply pick some quotes and copy them into their texts, but they also need to explain why the quote is in there. They have to really dig. Instead of just copying and pasting, they also need to explain what the quote means and let the reader know why it is included."

When it comes to addressing the challenges students experience in providing text-based evidence in constructed responses, Conestoga Valley School District in Lancaster, Pennsylvania, has discovered a simple writing formula that supports students in their writing of constructed response essays. According to curricular leader Michelle Trasborg, "The RACE writing formula has been transformational in supporting students to become focused and coherent writers while holding them accountable to successfully addressing the question in writing." The acronym RACE stands for four distinct tasks that writers are required to do. Its strengths also lie in the consistency with which it is used starting as early as 3rd grade and continuing through 12th grade in both the language arts as well as the content areas. The components of the RACE acronym are as follows:

R = **Read** the prompt and circle the key words and phrases that you want to use in your answer.

A = **Answer** the questions, using the key words and phrases that you circled.

(Younger students are asked to use as much of the question or prompt as possible in their answers.)

C = **Cite** examples straight from the text. Do this for each of your answers.

(Older students are asked to consolidate these from multiple sources.)

E = **Explain** how your citations help you prove your point. Do this for each of your citations.

While the acronym may sound simple, the power is in the way it requires students to cite evidence from the text and, most challenging of all, interpret that evidence for the reader. As students get older, the expectations become increasingly complex, using multiple sources of information. The framework, introduced by Michelle Trasborg, provides a scaffold for writing that necessitates that students find and interpret text-based evidence as support for their written response. According to Nicole Reinking, "RACE is so formulaic that with minimal instruction, children are able to pick it up and be successful."

By middle school the acronym becomes RACERS, with R and S standing for "Repeat Steps C and E." RACERS provides a guided step-by-step progression in the complexity of how to cite sources in order to bolster a point. Conestoga Valley teachers have used it successfully with students who are emerging as writers and with those who are in advanced writing classes. High school English teacher Melanie Upton noted, "What was really exciting was when I would see the RACE strategy filter into other things. Like on their selection tests, I would see the RACE letters at the top of the page, and they would ask, 'Can I use the RACE strategy on this?' When I walked around during their standardized testing last year, every student had the RACE checklist on the top of their pages, and their answers were amazing. We were really thrilled about how our open-ended scores turned out, and it's because of the RACE strategy." The teachers with whom we spoke all attributed higher test scores to their use of RACE.

Teaching the RACE formula

The R

Students are asked to carefully read a question or prompt. Teachers take time previewing and reviewing various types of questions. Students are taught to pay close attention to the verbs asking them to list, explain, analyze, and so forth.

The A

At the earlier grades students are asked to use as much of the original question as possible. At all grades, students are encouraged to note key phrases that must be addressed in their responses.

The C

Students are asked to locate and directly cite evidence from their texts.

The E

While a student's choice in using a certain citation may seem abundantly clear to them, the E requires that the students explain how the citation helps to support the point that they are making. In other words, it is not asking for a summary of the quote; it is asking the student to explain how the quote is an example of evidence supporting their response to the prompt.

To scaffold student success, teachers use a simple template that allows students to get started by filling out the basic components of RACE (see Figure 7.1). The templates are more sophisticated for older students. High school English teacher and curricular leader David Vega created a template (see Figure 7.2) to scaffold his high school students' success with the RACE formula. Notice the "Quick Citation Guide" at the bottom of the chart, which serves as a scaffold for students trying to add more sophistication to citations.

Modeling RACE

High school English teacher Katie Fake uses the familiar tale of Goldilocks to review the RACE framework (see Figure 7.3). She projects the document on the screen and reviews the components. Then she asks students

Figure 7.1

Basic RACE Writing Template

R
A   To do this, FLIP the _____[Question]_____ into a ___[Topic Sentence]_____ .
C   ***Be sure to ____[Cite]_____ all of your quotations, telling who said them and when.
E
REPEAT STEPS ___[C]___ and ____[E]____ , then conclude.

Template by Katie Fake. Used with permission.

to try to complete the RACE framework on their own. Once students are ready to review their work, Fake asks them to highlight the four components using designated highlighter colors. Fake notes that "it helps you diagnose where they are strong and any misunderstandings. Using the different colors, you can easily see where they think a citation would be explained, and you can show them what they need to do to improve their explanations. The highlighters help with the self-evaluation. And, the self-evaluation piece is critical." Fake notes that projecting the documents also plays a critical role in helping students evaluate sample works that would be strong, average, and weak. Annotations also occur during conferencing with the individual students.

Figure 7.2

David Vega's RACE Writing Template (high school)

	Answering the Essay Question/Prompt		
R	**Read the Question:** Circle the verbs in the prompt. Are you supposed to *explain, analyze, compare, contrast, discuss?* What aspect of the text is the question asking you to focus on?		
A	**Answer the question using a strong topic sentence.** Remember to mention the author and title of the reading selection, as well as answer the question.		
C	Cited Example 1:	Cited Example 2:	Cited Example 3:
E	Explanation for Ex 1:	Explanation for Ex 2:	Explanation for Ex 3:

Quick Citation Guide:
Use a signal phrase: *The author claims,* "quote." | *The character says,* "quote." | *The narrator/speaker argues,* "quote."

Simple Setup

☐ Ex. In line 17, **Stafford writes,** "I thought hard for us all."

☐ Ex. In line 17, **the speaker states,** "I thought hard for us all."

(Notice the comma comes after the signal phrase and the end period goes inside the quotation marks.)

Setup with Context Information

☐ Ex. Dying in the tall grass, his ankle swollen from the copperhead bite, Herman gasps, "I should have worn my boots." (Notice the context information **precedes** the signal phrase, which is followed by a comma.)

Created by David Vega, South Western High School. Used with permission.

Figure 7.3

Katie Fake's RACE with Goldilocks Example

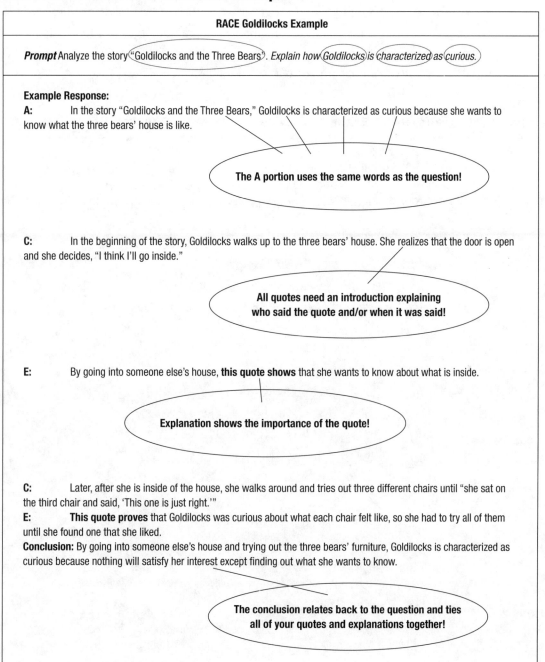

RACE Goldilocks Example

Prompt Analyze the story "Goldilocks and the Three Bears". *Explain how Goldilocks is characterized as curious.*

Example Response:

A: In the story "Goldilocks and the Three Bears," Goldilocks is characterized as curious because she wants to know what the three bears' house is like.

> The A portion uses the same words as the question!

C: In the beginning of the story, Goldilocks walks up to the three bears' house. She realizes that the door is open and she decides, "I think I'll go inside."

> All quotes need an introduction explaining who said the quote and/or when it was said!

E: By going into someone else's house, **this quote shows** that she wants to know about what is inside.

> Explanation shows the importance of the quote!

C: Later, after she is inside of the house, she walks around and tries out three different chairs until "she sat on the third chair and said, 'This one is just right.'"

E: **This quote proves** that Goldilocks was curious about what each chair felt like, so she had to try all of them until she found one that she liked.

Conclusion: By going into someone else's house and trying out the three bears' furniture, Goldilocks is characterized as curious because nothing will satisfy her interest except finding out what she wants to know.

> The conclusion relates back to the question and ties all of your quotes and explanations together!

Goldilocks example created by Katie Fake. Used with permission.

Figure 7.4 shows 6th grader Dylan's response to an open-ended prompt regarding NASA. Notice how he self-monitored his inclusion of the RACE components by adding the checked boxes on the left-hand side of the page. seventh grader Anna's example begins with a graphic organizer that helps her prepare through a prewrite (see Figure 7.5). Her finished product embeds all of the elements from her prewrite into a fluid essay (see Figure 7.6).

Figure 7.4

Dylan's (6th grade) RACE Example with Self-Monitoring Checked Boxes

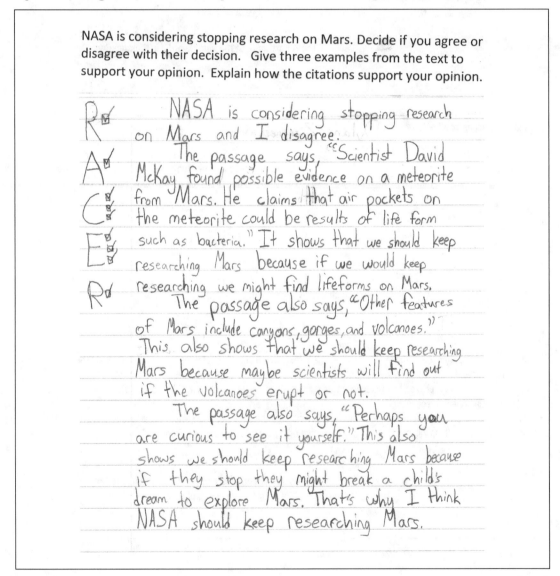

NASA is considering stopping research on Mars. Decide if you agree or disagree with their decision. Give three examples from the text to support your opinion. Explain how the citations support your opinion.

R☑ NASA is considering stopping research on Mars and I disagree.

A☑ The passage says, "Scientist David McKay found possible evidence on a meteorite

C☑ from Mars. He claims that air pockets on the meteorite could be results of life form

E☑ such as bacteria." It shows that we should keep researching Mars because if we would keep

R☑ researching we might find lifeforms on Mars. The passage also says, "Other features of Mars include canyons, gorges, and volcanoes." This also shows that we should keep researching Mars because maybe scientists will find out if the volcanoes erupt or not. The passage also says, "Perhaps you are curious to see it yourself." This also shows we should keep researching Mars because if they stop they might break a child's dream to explore Mars. That's why I think NASA should keep researching Mars.

Figure 7.5

Anna's (7th grade) Prewrite

<table>
<tr><td></td><td>Name: Anna</td></tr>
<tr><td></td><td>Period: 7</td></tr>
</table>

RACERS pre-writing

Read the question and circle/highlight key words:

How does Major Morris feel about the monkey's paw? Give two examples from the story that support your answer. Make sure you explain how your examples support your answer.

Answer by restating: Major Morris feels very frightened at the very thought of the Monkey's Paw and regretful for using it

Cite (Example 1 from text): ___(page #) "I have" face whitened.

Explain how example supports your answer: Nervous or scared - face whitening

Repeat:

Cite _(page #) "If you had another three wishes, would you use them?" Response throw paw in fire

Explain Want it to burn because of horrible things, ~~Regrets~~ using it

Summarize by restating topic sentence: By his face whitening at the mere mention of the paw and throwing the paw into the fire, shows that Major Morris is frightened of the paw and regrets using it.

Figure 7.6

Anna's Finished Product

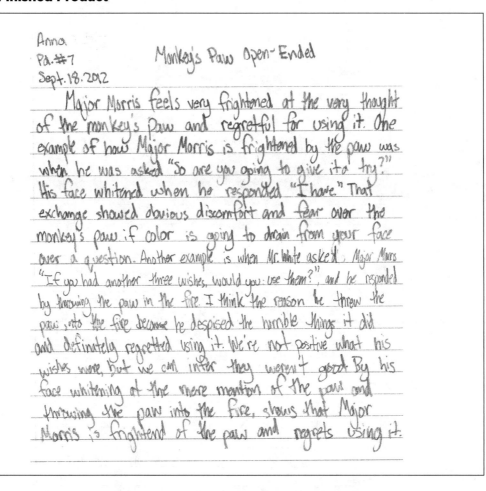

Anna
Pd. #7
Sept. 18, 2012

Monkey's Paw Open-Ended

Major Morris feels very frightened at the very thought of the monkey's paw and regretful for using it. One example of how Major Morris is frightened by the paw was when he was asked "So are you going to give it a try?" His face whitened when he responded "I have." That exchange showed obvious discomfort and fear over the monkey's paw if color is going to drain from your face over a question. Another example is when Mr. White asked, Major Morris "If you had another three wishes, would you use them?", and he responded by throwing the paw in the fire. I think the reason he threw the paw into the fire because he despised the horrible thing it did and definitely regretted using it. We're not positive what his wishes were, but we can infer they weren't good. By his face whitening at the mere mention of the paw and throwing the paw into the fire, shows that Major Morris is frightened of the paw and regrets using it.

The Challenge of Responding to the E

According to Trasborg, the E is always the most difficult of the four components because the students can't simply summarize their citation. "They have to tie the quotes back to the original prompt. For example, students might say, 'This quote proves that . . . .' In order to complete the E, they have to explain the relationship between the text-based evidence and the prompt. Students must elaborate and explain this relationship by giving their interpretation of the citation and draw the connection back to the essence of the question. It sounds simple, but it's really the most difficult piece for them."As students get older, they progress in their sophistication of how they explain their thinking. What is accepted by 3rd grade teachers as sufficient evidence becomes more complex in later years. Sentence fluency and author's voice become more nuanced as students gain greater experience with reading and writing. According to Trasborg, as students progress through the grades, the E's become more sophisticated, and we work on introducing citations in a more subtle format." Figure 7.7 provides a simple chart showing sample progressions of explanations that are based on the same citation.

Figure 7.7

Examples of Progressions of Explanations

C: **Citation**	According to the author, "Michaela looked into the audience, and finished her speech with a confident bow."
E: **Incomplete Explanation** (Incomplete, because it doesn't explain how what you're saying is true.)	When Michaela gave her speech it showed that she had changed.
E: **Acceptable Explanation for the early intermediate grades** (It provides a general explanation that what you're saying is true.)	When Michaela gave her speech it showed that she had changed because in the beginning of the story she had been terrified of speaking.
E: **Evidence-based Explanation for adolescents.** (It provides specific, text-based evidence that what you're saying is true.)	When Michaela gave her speech it showed that she had changed because in the beginning of the story, she had been terrified of speaking. She was even too afraid to talk to the store clerk. Giving a speech in front of the school showed that she had conquered that fear.
E: **Evidence-based Explanation demonstrating college-ready attributes** (It provides specific, text-based evidence that what you're saying is true, and does so without choppy language that makes readers feel like they're reading a test booklet response.)	Michaela's growing courage was demonstrated by the author's use of events in her life that showed that she had progressed from one who was deathly afraid of the simplest of conversations, such as her inability to talk to the store clerk, to her brave presentation of the graduation speech in front of hundreds of students.

Scoring RACE essays

Teachers included various nuances to their scoring tool or rubrics that allowed them to focus on specific focal points within their classes. Where writing conclusions is concerned, 7th grade reading teacher Victoria Henderson allows students to simply restate their topic sentence for the beginning of the year. But as time evolves, she assigns full credit only to those who go beyond restating their topic by also briefly recapping their evidence. These expectations are spelled out in her scoring tool (see Figure 7.8). According to Henderson, "it's hard to conference with 150 students, so if students know where they went wrong by looking at the scoring tool, and they want to resubmit their papers, I'll let them do that. Sometimes they completely forget to explain, and they'll lose enough points so that it is not considered proficient. The scoring tool allows them to know where they lost the points." Figure 7.9 provides a rubric with qualitative features spelled out for students.

High school English teacher and curricular leader David Vega created a more sophisticated rubric (see Figure 7.10) for scaffolding student success. According to Vega, "students at first struggle to move beyond the developing level because they are so conditioned to memorize and regurgitate information rather than applying, analyzing, and evaluating ideas. As students experience multiple exposures and receive continual feedback, their scores and thinking improve significantly." Vega teaches older learners, and his focus is college readiness. As a result, his rubric expects a certain degree of sophistication from student writings.

Figure 7.8
Simple 10-Point Scoring System

Name_____

Read the question carefully.
___ /2 **Answer** by restating the question and including your answer.
___ /1 **Cite** example #1 from the text.
___ /2 **Explain** how citation/example supports your answer.
    Repeat
    ___ /1 **Cite** example #2 from the text.
    ___ /2 **Explain** how the 2nd citation/example supports the answer.
    ___ /2 **Summarize** with a concluding sentence that wraps up your answer and your evidence.

Created by Victoria Henderson. Used with permission.

Figure 7.9

RACE Rubric with Qualitative Descriptions

Criterion	5 = Advanced	4 = Proficient	3 = Basic	2 = Below Basic
A—Answer	Provides a **correct** response by writing **to the prompt**	Provides a **plausible** response that **attempts to address the prompt**	Provides a **limited** response	Provides a **superficial and/or incorrect** response
C—Citing Quotations	Cites **specific and appropriate examples**	Cites **general and relevant examples** from text OR Cites **specific but weak** examples	Cites **little and/or irrelevant evidence**	Cites no evidence
E—Explanation and Elaboration	Provides **substantial elaboration or explanation;** shows deep comprehension; **makes specific and sophisticated connections**	Provides **adequate elaboration or explanation;** attempts to comprehend beyond the literal; **makes general but relevant connections**	Exhibits mostly a **literal and/or surface level** comprehension; makes irrelevant connections, at best	Exhibits **little or no comprehension;** makes **no connections**
Writing Skills	Displays **excellent writing skills** (0–2 errors).	Displays **adequate writing skills.** Few errors (3–4).	Displays **weak writing skills**. Many errors (4 or more).	Displays writing deficiency. Errors hinder the reading.

Created by Susan Grammer and Katie Fake. Used with permission.

What About the Content-Area Classes?

While the RACE strategy doesn't fit with every open-ended prompt, it does prepare students to provide evidence for their thinking in prompts that require students to provide text-based evidence. Its use across disciplines sets an expectation for students to not just state what they've learned, but also to explain why it helps prove their point. Seventh grade science teacher Ramón Rivera appreciates the fact that the strategy provides these expectations, because he only needs to reference it. According to Rivera, "We try to write a RACE question for

Figure 7.10

Vega's RACE Rubric (high school)

Responding to Literature

Student: _____ Score = 4 | 3.5 | 3 | 2.5 | 2 | 1.5 | 1.0

Response to _____

Criterion	4 = Advanced	3 = Proficient	2 = Developing	1 = Beginning
Accuracy	Provides either a correct or logically plausible response that directly addresses the prompt	Provides a plausible response (with few if any errors) that addresses the prompt	Provides an incorrect response (with egregious errors and/or flawed thinking) that attempts to address the prompt	Provides a superficial, flawed, and/or incorrect response
Supporting Evidence	Cites specific, carefully selected text examples that advance an argument	Cites general and/or relevant (though not the most appropriate or logical) text examples that support the answer	Cites little and/or irrelevant text examples that attempt to support the answer	Cites irrelevant or no evidence from text
Commentary and Elaboration **Weight (X2)**	Provides substantial elaboration and forceful explanations that show a sophisticated understanding of the text/s; makes sophisticated connections that move the response into *analysis, synthesis,* or *evaluation*	Provides adequate elaboration and clear explanations that show a working understanding of the text/s; demonstrates a clear attempt to move response beyond *application* and *interpretation* levels; makes general but relevant connections	Exhibits mostly a literal and/or surface level comprehension; displays ability to *recall* or *apply* ideas and/or skills, although with some limitations; makes obvious or irrelevant connections	Exhibits little or no comprehension; makes no meaningful connections

Created by David Vega, South Western High School. Used with permission.

each unit. I think it's a good way for them to demonstrate what they've learned. It's easy to use. The students know the format. I'll say, 'I want this in a RACE format,' and they already know what that means."

RACE isn't just for referencing knowledge gained from texts. When Rivera asks students to cite sources, he is making reference to citing knowledge gained from any mode of lesson delivery that was used in his science class. Rivera expects students to reflect back on these sources of learning when they respond to his prompts. "The difference with my use of RACE is that instead of citing from a book, they're citing evidence that they've learned in class through demonstrations, projects, and lecture presentations. I might use a prompt where they're asked to classify a type of plant, and I'll give them certain information. Their evidence cited will be based on what they have learned about plants as opposed to text citations. They are still required to cite the supporting evidence."

It is important to note that writing in response to prompts cannot be the only type of writing that students do in school. If all students ever learn is this type of writing, and this type of reading, we fail to extract the most powerful opportunities that literature and informational texts have to offer students as thinkers, as analytical meaning makers, and as future adults. At the same time, we are faced with the responsibility of equipping students with the tools to survive and thrive in an educational environment that relies heavily on students' abilities to effectively substantiate claims based on what they read. For teachers looking for a simple formula that will help them articulate how to address constructed response essay prompts, RACE can provide that simple pointed support for helping students coherently respond to prompts using text-based evidence.

8

Conclusion: Growing Thinkers, Readers, and Writers

Reading and celebrating words has to be authentic. It has to be driven by the portions of the book that move the emotions: motivation, joy, engagement, and love of real, authentic reading.
—Keely Potter, Master Teacher and 5th–8th Grade Language Arts teacher

Preparing students to independently and critically read grade-level literature and informational texts will require that we help students fall in love with reading. It will take an intentional and strategic focus on celebrating words within contexts that are authentic and that drive students to want to celebrate words. The way we approach learning is critical; we have to help our students want to learn, and the right tools can help us do that. We're asking a lot of our students. Proficiency in the use of words is an ongoing process. It won't happen overnight, and it won't happen without an understanding of the interconnectedness of listening, speaking, reading, and writing, or the importance of well-structured interactions around text.

In this book, we explore many elements of literacy and provide various tools or techniques for focusing on the following important features of engaging readers as thinkers:

- **Academic language** is quantifiably complicated. There are specific features that make it complicated, and there are ways that we can support students through their acquisition of academic language. We present tools for supporting the acquisition of academic language as more than just learning isolated vocabulary words.
- **Literature** helps students develop academic language in ways that are enjoyable. Literature also presents us with numerous opportunities for helping students develop their higher-order thinking skills, by helping

students focus on analyzing, synthesizing, and evaluating texts and author-related aspects of the texts. Researchers continue to unearth benefits associated with leisure reading. We have provided tools for using literature to develop academic language and to help students develop as critical thinkers.

- **Helping students engage deeply with text** takes an intentional, purposeful pausing to analyze various features regarding how and why the text was written. Students can be made explicitly aware of the differences between lower- and higher-order thinking so that they can analyze the cognitive intensity of their work. We encourage teachers to help students in making this distinction, and we have provided tools that we hope will be beneficial for this purpose.

- **We can help students develop a literary life of their own.** We can guide them toward developing a vibrant reading history. It will take an intentional analysis of where they are and what they need. It will also take getting to know them on a more personal level through talking to them about books. We do not believe that this can happen through traditional lecture hall approaches to teaching reading, or through small-group isolated drill-and-kill approaches to teaching reading. The affective and emotional connectedness needs to be present. Teaching reading is more than teaching isolated skills to students—we are helping them to understand themselves and their worlds through the power of words. We have provided tools for helping students develop a literary life of their own.

- **Helping students navigate the language of informational texts** needs to be an intentional focus in our schools. Passive reading is not only ineffective—it also promotes a gullible complacency that may prove dangerous in the long run. We need to help students in their development as analytical and active reviewers of what they read. We have provided tools for helping students be successful with reading and analyzing informational texts.

- **Classrooms must be safe and accepting environments** that allow students to take risks. Our students are developing higher-order thinking skills. This is an active and interactive process. Along the way, they need to feel like they can take risks and share textual interpretations without fear of being ostracized. We have provided a few

Total Participation Techniques and tools for supporting the development of classrooms where students interact around the text.

- **Providing text-based evidence** is a skill that can be strategically taught. The tendency for students to "freeze up" and become overwhelmed when faced with a constructed response essay prompt that requires text-based evidence can be overcome with the right scaffolds. We present a tool that is currently being used successfully within a local school district.

Overall, we approach learning as an interconnected process that involves *listening* to academic language within meaningful contexts; *reading* academic language and celebrating words for the meanings they capture; *talking* about academic language and the authors' uses of it; *thinking* about and analyzing texts that present academic language in beautiful and purposeful ways—and, in turn, *writing* about text-based interpretations as a form of celebrating our discoveries; *sharing* new discoveries gained through our analysis of text; and *writing* about texts in ways that are cogent and comprehensible. Our hope is that teachers find the various tools within this text to be helpful in supporting their students along their literary journeys; that students will discover that there are whole new ways of looking at life, understanding themselves, and understanding their worlds; and that these learning experiences can all be accessed through the pages of books.

Appendix: Annotated Bibliography of Books Featuring Academic Language and an Appreciation for Words

Contributed by:

Dr. Lesley Colabucci, Associate Professor specializing in children's literature, Millersville University

Dr. Jennifer Shettel, Associate Professor specializing in literacy methods, Millersville University

This appendix contains a list of carefully selected books that reflect a high quality in terms of literary merit and overall aesthetic appeal. The list offers a balance of selections from picture books through young adult novels. Each piece represents the best in terms of literary elements as well as in writing style. They would make suitable read-alouds at the appropriate age levels.

The books were selected based on a variety of criteria including such aspects as newer publication dates, substantial multicultural content, and "hidden gems" (books that were well reviewed but seem to have not made it into classrooms). In addition, many of the books feature characters who have a love of words or a command of academic language. Not only do the authors offer opportunities to appreciate the beauty of language, but the very content of the stories sometimes focus on the character's reflections on the power of literacy.

Multicultural Emphasis

Johnson, A. (2003). *The First Part Last*. New York: Simon & Schuster.

• Grades 7–12, 132 pages, 790 Lexile

Situated as a prequel, this book tells the back story behind how teenager Bobby came to be a single father. Told in short poetic chapters, the plot unfolds in a back-and-forth style so that readers are kept wondering what happens to the baby's mother as well as the extended families on both sides. Bobby's identity development, complicated family dynamics, and the challenges and joys of the urban context are all explored in this subtly beautiful novel.

> *Feather sleeps like these kittens I saw once at a farm my summer camp went to. They were all curled up in an old crate, sleeping with paws on their brothers and sisters. Sleeping safe and with family.* (p. 8)

Joseph, L. (2000). *The Color of My Words.* **New York: HarperCollins Children's Books.**

• Grades 6–9, 144 pages, 840 Lexile

Ana Rosa lives in a poor village in the Dominican Republic and dreams of becoming a writer because of how she experiences the emotional power of words. Caught in political and cultural upheaval, Ana Rosa overcomes great personal tragedy in order to celebrate the beauty around her and seek empowerment for herself and her community through her own writing.

> *Papi might sound as if he is talking in a puzzle, but I always know exactly what he means. Like when I asked him if I could have a notebook just for writing my poems in. He said, "Muchacha, your head is getting bigger than your hat."* (p. 16)

Lai, T. (2011). *Inside Out and Back Again* **New York: HarperCollins.**

• Grades 3–7, 288 pages, 800 Lexile

This novel, written in verse, captures the experience—both personal and academic—of a young girl who emigrates from Vietnam because of the war. From the boat journey to settling in at school in Alabama, Ha and her family (her mother and three brothers) experience life as refugees, suffering alienation and bullying. They find support from teachers and neighbors along the way. The following excerpt exemplifies some of the assimilation struggles portrayed in this book.

> *Fire hair on skin dotted with spots.*
>
> *Fuzzy dark hair on skin shiny as lacquer.*
> *Hair the color of root on milky skin.*

Lots of braids on milk chocolate.
White hair on a pink boy.
Honey hair with orange ribbons on see-through skin.
Hair with barrettes in all colors on bronze bread.
I'm the only
Straight black hair
on olive skin. (p. 142)

Ryan, P. M. (2010). *The Dreamer.* New York: Scholastic.

• Grades 4 and up, 400 pages, 650 Lexile

This book explores the childhood of Pablo Neruda, a 20th century poet, and the difficult relationship he had with his father. Neftalí, the young boy in the story, longs to write and is constantly thinking of words. His father feels that this passion is a waste of time and demands that Neftalí prepare for a very different career as a businessman. Despite this conflict, Neftalí holds on tightly to his dreams and continues to have hope in his heart. The excerpt below demonstrates the poetic and sensory-filled style of the author. This passage describes how Neftalí cannot escape his need to write and imagine, even when he puts his notebook away in his drawer:

> *The words he had written wiggled off the page and escaped from the drawer. The letters stacked themselves, one on top of the other. Their towers reached higher and higher until they stood majestic and tall, surrounding Neftalí in a city of promise.* (p. 299)

Sloan, H. G. (2012). *Counting by Sevens.* New York: Dial.

• Grades 5–8, 378 pages, 650 Lexile

This character-driven novel follows Willow Chance as she forges new friendships and finds a way to rebuild her life after a family tragedy. Each character's perspective is shared in different sections of the narrative, but it's Willow's intelligence and quirky interests that readers will remember. Willow is a thinker at heart and models mathematical, creative, and logical reasoning as she navigates her new life.

> *Camouflage is a form of crypsis, which means hiding. The skin on my ankles is dark and I'm wearing a pair of work boots. The carpeting here is also shades of tan and chocolate. It is a pattern of swirls and dots, no doubt*

installed to camouflage any dirt. I'm hiding in plain sight which is often the best way to be concealed. (p. 153)

New Classics

Birdsall, J. (2005). *The Penderwicks: A Summer Tale of Four Sisters, Two Rabbits, and a Very Interesting Boy.* **New York: Knopf.**

• Grades 3–7, 272 pages, 800 Lexile

A charming story of four sisters and their widowed father who spend their summer by the sea. Described by readers as an "old-fashioned kind of story" with no references to pop culture or modern-day issues, this is a domestic tale exploring friendships and celebrating family closeness in a text rich with descriptive language.

> *All was at peace while Batty picked flowers and hummed a song about kangaroos. Above, the birds wheeled cheerfully across the sky. Below, the worms slid happily through the soil. In between, the summer breeze softly ruffled the clover and daisies.* (p. 55)

Ellsworth, L. (2007). *In Search of Mockingbird.* **New York: Holt.**

• Grades 5–9, 192 pages, 680 Lexile

Sixteen-year-old Erin's story functions as homage to the classic *To Kill a Mockingbird.* Erin is obsessed with both the novel and its author, as was her own deceased mother. The plot revolves around Erin's family struggles and her attempt to connect in person with Harper Lee. This story models the effect a single book can have on a life. The excerpt below shows Erin in conversation with another traveler to whom she has revealed her goal of meeting the famous author:

> *We're both quiet for a long moment, listening to the gibberish of voices blended with loud music blaring from the bar. Epp appears lost in thought. "I think the trip has more meaning than you realize," he finally says as though he's convinced himself of the fact, "but what if Harper Lee won't talk with you?" My hand voluntarily pats down the cover of "Mockingbird," I push my finger against a small tear at the lower front corner of the jacket. "I've thought about that. You remember how Atticus lost his case? He said there's honor in trying. There's even honor in defeat.* (p. 114)

Hannigan, K. (2004). *Ida B. and Her Plans to Maximize Fun, Avoid Disaster, and (Possibly) Save the World.* **New York: Greenwillow.**

• Grades 3 and up, 272 pages, 970 Lexile

Upon being forced to attend public school after having been homeschooled by her mother, Ida resists everything from making friends to embracing her love of reading. Great characterization marks this book, and Ida's attitude and actions may both repel and appeal to young readers. Ida is a testament to the power of reading as we cope with questions, change, and tragedy in our lives.

> So I was thinking I would save a lot of time and energy if I could figure out a way to keep my face clean, and The Soap Mask is what I came up with. "An impenetrable wall of disinfectant for your face." "A shield that repels germs while it gently cleanses your pores, leaving a spanking-clean exterior." "External, perpetual, ultimate cleanliness." That's what the advertisements would say, I was thinking, when I put it on the market and sold ten million of them. (p. 21)

Kelly, J. (2012). *Return to the Willows.* **New York: Holt.**

• Grades 2–6. 288 pages, 890 Lexile

Author Jacqueline Kelly writes a sequel to the beloved Kenneth Grahame book *The Wind in the Willows* (published in 1908). A testament to how a book as timeless as Grahame's can inspire writers more than 100 years later, this book is full of playful dialogue and classic animal adventure, complemented by lush watercolor paintings. Friendship, language, and nature are celebrated throughout.

> The Mole had brought along a good book to read (for it is a firm and fast rule that one should never leave one's burrow without a good book in hand) and was deeply immersed in the adventures of a young girl who'd fallen down a rabbit hole. The hole was unlike any the Mole had ever visited—and he had visited any number of them in his time, for he counted a great many rabbits among his friends—but he was enjoying it immensely, as he was very fond of all stories that took place underground. He leaned back upon a plump cushion and wiggled his toes in sheer happiness. (p. 2)

McNeal, T. (2013). *Far, Far Away.* **New York: Random House.**

• Grades 9–12, 224 pages, 790 Lexile

Set in the town of Never Better, teenager Jeremy Johnson Johnson is trying to help his ailing father make ends meet in order to keep their house. Add to this a mysterious baker, a troublesome girl, and the ghost of fairy-tale writer Jacob Grimm and you have a story in which dreaming of life in a kingdom "far, far away" isn't out of the question. A slightly creepy mystery novel that older teens will enjoy.

> *Let us begin on a May afternoon when the light was pure, the air scented with blossoms and the sky a pale blue. Lovely, in other words, and brimming with promise. The village trees were in full leaf, and there, in the town square, under the shade of one such tree, a boy named Jeremy Johnson Johnson stood surrounded by three girls.* (p. 1)

Ritter, J. (2003). *The Boy Who Saved Baseball.* New York: Philomel.

• Grades 4 and up, 224 pages, 660 Lexile

Dillontown will lose its beloved baseball field unless Tom Gallagher can figure out a way to save it. With themes of determination, hope, and—of course—baseball, this book holds universal appeal for readers.

> *A boy needs to read the earth. This is a truth older than the iron dust that redpaints the boulders. It's older than the woolback mammoths that're fossilized in these hills. It's a feeling truth, a gut truth formed deep inside, that leads a boy to bouldertops on mountaintops, scanning ancient vistas, listening like a perched hawk, reading willow trees for buried water, canyonsides for fruit or meat, and the ridgetops for friend or stranger.* (p. 59)

Poetry

Engle, M. (2006). *Poet Slave of Cuba.* New York: Holt.

• Grades 6 and up

This novel in verse combines poetry and biography, chronicling the life of Juan Francisco Manzano. While the time and the place (Cuba in the early 1800s) may be unfamiliar to readers, they will be able connect this story to other slave narratives. However, Juan's story will stand out both because of how it is told through poetry and because of the level of degradation and struggle described. Engle gives readers information about Juan and his childhood and young adulthood alongside access to his poetic voice. The use of multiple narrators will engage readers throughout the journey that takes place in the book.

> *I feel like a homing pigeon*
> *longing for my dovecote*
> *Havana is in my heart*
> *city of poets*
> *city of freedom*
> *streets of words*
> *alleys of wonder* (p. 160)

Grandits, J. (2007). *Blue Lipstick.* **New York: Clarion Books.**

• Grades 6 and up

This collection of concrete poetry is targeted at preteen and young adults. Subjects include zombie jocks, bad hair days, and volleyball practice. While many of the poems offer reflections on everyday life, others offer opportunities for content connections as well as critical thinking. For instance, the poem "Mondrian" explores art, while others build vocabulary (*phrenology*, for instance, in the poem "Science"). While teen angst is a dominant theme, a love of words and poetry also pervades the collection.

> *Angels*
> *Metaphysical mysteries*
> *unconditional forgiveness*
> *Friendly attitudes*
> *good will*
> *Charitable actions*
> *good will*
> *Helpful advice*
> *Unusual tolerance* (p. 24)

Hopkins, L. B. (2004). *Wonderful Words: Poems About Reading, Writing, Speaking, and Listening* **(Illus. K. Barbour). New York: Simon & Schuster.**

• Grades 1–5

This essence of this book is the importance and beauty of communication. The poems range in tone; some are playful and funny, while others passionately reflect on the joy of creating on paper ("Writing Past Midnight") and engaging with story ("Share the Adventure"). The poem "Scout's Honor" reveals the spirit of this collection and the potential for exploring language:

I tripped,
humiliated by
a loose lace.
Laughter scarred
every single face
but yours.
Scouts honor
I'll carry your backpack
forever. (p. 20)

Nye, N. S. (2002). *19 Varieties of Gazelle: Poems of the Middle East.* New York: Greenwillow Books.

• Grades 6 and up

Through 60 poems, this collection explores various facets of life as an Arab American. The poems do not avoid controversy and reflect a depth of cultural knowledge and experience. Nye's poems are characterized by emotional force and sophisticated use of imagery. Throughout this collection, characters and places are introduced that will be unfamiliar to some readers. This provides an opportunity for learning and reflecting on one's own culture and context.

Olive Jar
In the corner of every Arab kitchen,
an enormous plastic container
of olives is waiting for another meal.
Green tight-skinned olives
planets with slightly pointed ends—
after breakfast, lunch, each plate
hosts a pyramid of pits in one corner. (p. 80)

Sidman, J. (2007). *This Is Just to Say: Poems of Apology and Forgiveness* (Illus by P. Zagorinski). Boston: Houghton Mifflin.

• Grades 1–5

As indicated by the title, the book is inspired by the famous poem by William Carlos Williams. Each selection portrays interactions in narrative form as children and adults apologize for actions (such as stealing donuts) and find their way to forgiveness. The poems ring with authenticity and capture the voice of the fictionalized speaker in ways that will resonate with young readers.

> Here I am
> reading Mai Lee's poem.
> I am wading into the river of forgiveness…
> Thinking . . . of confusion,
> and the fear that crushes your heart
> when you've done something wrong…

Narrative Nonfiction

Hoose, P. (2012). *Moonbird: A Year on the Wind with the Great Survivor B95.* New York: Farrar, Straus, & Giroux.

• Grades 4–8, 160 pages, 1150 Lexile

A great book to accompany a unit on extinct or endangered species. Hoose details the story of one small bird—a 4-ounce Rufa nicknamed "Moonbird" by the scientists who have been tracking him for the past 20 years because the distance he has flown is equivalent to the distance between the Earth and the moon and back again—using a model for expository writing that is both engaging and informative.

> At nightfall, constellations of the northern sky fade behind them and new star clusters take their place in the southern sky ahead. After a third continuous day and night of exertion, B95's feathers are worn and frayed. His wing tendons are stressed almost to the tearing point, and he is panting for oxygen. But the flock pushes on, at last entering tropical latitudes, where it receives a welcome boost from warm trade winds that blow stiffly from the northeast. (p. 103)

Hopkinson, D. (2012). *Titanic: Voices from the Disaster.* New York: Scholastic.

• Grades 4–8, 304 pages, 1040 Lexile

Hopkinson combines letters, photographs, and other primary source documents to present the historical account of the sinking of the *Titanic* in a gripping format. This book is an excellent example of the use of primary source, historical accuracy, and multiple perspectives.

> *The loss of life was heartbreaking. It seems unbelievable even today. How did this magnificent ship, the largest and most luxurious in the world, simply disappear in a matter of hours?* (p. 8)

Sheinkin, S. (2012). *Bomb: The Race to Build—and Steal—the World's Most Dangerous Weapon.* New York: Roaring Book Press.

- Grades 5–9, 266 pages, 920 Lexile

Sheinkin uses an engaging narrative style to pull the reader into the excellent nonfiction account of the world race to build the atomic bomb. Sheinkin combines a number of sources into a riveting story that reads like a mystery novel but is 100% true. For classes studying World War II, this book will add to the discussion by adding a whole new layer.

> *Robert Oppenheimer wanted the job. Oppenheimer first met Groves on October 8, on the Berkeley campus. Groves was traveling around the country, meeting people who'd been working on the Uranium Committee. He and Oppenheimer chatted at lunch, then Oppenheimer invited Groves back to his office for a longer talk.*
>
> *Oppenheimer laid out his vision for getting the bomb built. Work was being done at universities all over the country, he told Groves. Scientists were wasting time doing the same things on different campuses. And, because of security worries, they weren't allowed to share information over the phone or by mail. That had to end.* (p. 48)

Silvey, A. (2012). *The Plant Hunters: True Stories of Their Daring Adventures to the Far Corners of the Earth.* New York: Farrar, Straus, & Giroux.

- Grades 4–9, 96 pages, 1170 Lexile

A perfect read-aloud for biology teachers, this book explores the lives of both early and modern-day "plant hunters"—adventurous scientists who scour the Earth to discover new or previously undiscovered species of plants and bring them back to their home countries.

Those who survived endured all kinds of challenges. Vampire bats sucked on their toes; bears attacked them in the woods. These intrepid adventurers faced slime pits, snowdrifts, river rapids, floods, and avalanches. They fell into fitful sleep at night in jungles, listening to the deafening chattering and screeching of wild animals. The sun burned them by day; the cold seeped into their bones at night. They were racked by fever.

Who were these adventurers? They were not soldiers or pirates; they followed a profession with zeal, but were not missionaries, doctors, or spies. They had a different purpose, a very dangerous mission. They risked their lives to find something seemingly ordinary: plants. (p. 3)

Walker, S. (2012). *Blizzard of Glass: The Halifax Explosion of 1917.* New York: Holt.

• Grades 5–9, 160 pages, 1100 Lexile

Told in vivid detail and supported with photographs and extensive documentation, this is the little-known story of a ship collision that left 2,000 people dead and flattened two towns in Canada in 1917. Connections can be made to other disasters—both natural and man-made, in more recent history.

As countries in Europe began challenging each other for control of territory, they amassed armies that grew even larger. Suspicions and mistrust escalated to a fever pitch as countries formed alliances with one another. An alliance is an agreement between countries that joins them together for a purpose, often to wage war. (p. 3)

References

Anderson, L. W., & Krathwohl, D. R. (Eds.). (2001). *A taxonomy for learning, teaching, and assessing: A revision of Bloom's taxonomy of educational objectives.* New York: Longman.

Austen, J. (2012, first published in 1813). *Pride and prejudice.* New York: Fall River Press.

Beck, I. L., & McKeown, M. G. (2007). Increasing young low income children's oral vocabulary repertoires through rich and focused instruction. *Elementary School Journal, 107*(3), 251–271.

Beck, I. L., McKeown, M. G., & Kucan, L. (2002). *Bringing words to life: Robust vocabulary instruction.* New York: Guilford Press.

Beers, K. (1998, April). Listen while you read: Struggling readers and audiobooks. *School Library Journal*, pp. 30–35.

Berns, G. S., Blaine, K., Prietula, M. J., & Pye, B. E. (2013). Short-and long-term effects of a novel on connectivity in the brain. *Brain Connectivity, 3*(6), 590–600.

Biemiller, A., & Boote, C. (2006). An effective method for building meaning vocabulary in primary grades *Journal of Educational Psychology, 98*(1), 44–62.

Biemiller, A., & Slonim, N. (2001). Estimating root word vocabulary growth in normative and advantaged populations: Evidence for a common sequence of vocabulary acquisition. *Journal of Educational Psychology, 93*(3), 498–520.

Biemiller, A. (2003). Vocabulary: Needed if more children are to read well. *Reading Psychology, 24*, 323–335.

Bloom, B. S. (1956). *Taxonomy of educational objectives: The classification of educational goals. Handbook 1, Cognitive domain.* New York: Longmans, Green.

Bomar, L. (2006, May/June). Ipods as reading tools. *Principal* (NAESP National Association of Elementary School Principals).

Brown, A. C., & Schulten, K. (2010, March 4). What's your reading history? Reflecting on the self as reader. *New York Times, The Learning Network: Teaching & Learning with the New York Times,* http://learning.blogs.nytimes.com/2010/03/04/whats-your-reading-history-reflecting-on-the-self-as-reader/?_r = 0

Cardillo, A., Coville, B., Ditlow, T., Myrick, E., & Lesesne, T. (2007). Tuning in to audiobooks: Why should kids listen? *Children and Libraries: The Journal of the Association for Library Service to Children. 5*(3), 42–46.

Carlo, M. S., August, D., McLaughlin, B., Snow, C. E., Dressler, C., Lippman, D. N., et al. (2004). Closing the gap: Addressing the vocabulary needs of English language learners in bilingual and mainstream classrooms. *Reading Research Quarterly, 39*(2), 188–215.

Cunningham, A. E., & Stanovich, K. E. (2001). What reading does for the mind. *Journal of Direct Instruction, 1*(2), 137–149.

Dahl, R. (1961). *James and the giant peach.* New York: Puffin Books.

Davidson, J. W., & Stoff, M.B. (2007). *America: History of our nation, beginnings to 1914* (Pennsylvania edition). Boston: Prentice Hall.

DiCamillo, K. (2003). *The tale of Desperaux.* New York: Scholastic.

Dickens, C. (2012, first published in 1859). *A tale of two cities*. New York: Simon & Brown.

Dickinson, D. K., & Porche, M. V. (2011, May–June). Relation between language experiences in preschool classrooms and children's kindergarten and fourth-grade language and reading abilities. *Child Development, 82*(3), 870–886.

Elley, W. B. (1989). Vocabulary acquisition from listening to stories. *Reading Research Quarterly, 24*(2), 174–187.

Elley, W. B. (1991, September). Acquiring literacy in a second language: The effect of book-based programs. *Language Learning, 41*(3), 375–411.

Elley, W. B. (2000, July). The potential of book floods for raising literacy levels. *International Review of Education, 46*(3/4), 233–255.

Elley, W. B., & Mangubhai, F. (1983). The impact of reading on second language learning. *Reading Research Quarterly, 19*(1), 53–67.

EPE (2013). *Findings from a national survey of teacher perspectives on the Common Core*. Bethesda, MD: Educational Projects in Education Research Center.

Ferlazzo, L. (2013, January 12). EdWeek blog: Classroom Q & A with Larry Ferlazzo: http://blogs.edweek.org/teachers/classroom_qa_with_larry_ferlazzo/2013/01/response_ways_to_deal_with_history_myths_in_the_classroom.html

Funke, C. (2003). *Inkheart*. New York: Scholastic, Chicken House.

Gallo, D. R. (2007). *First crossing: Stories about teen immigrants*. London: Candlewick Press.

Gambrell, L. B., Wilson, R. M., & Gantt, W. N. (2001). Classroom observations of task-attending behaviors of good and poor readers. *Journal of Educational Research, 74*(6), 400–404.

Goos, M., Galbraith, P., & Renshaw, P. (2002). Socially mediated metacognition: Creating collaborative zones of proximal development in small group problem solving. *Educational Studies in Mathematics, 49*(2), 193–223.

Gross, S. M. (2013, June 6). *Beyond the book: Infographics of students' reading history*. Edutopia Blog, http://www.edutopia.org/blog/infographics-students-reading-history-sarah-gross

Güvenç, H., & Ün Açikgöz, K. (2007). The effects of cooperative learning and concept mapping on learning strategy use. *Educational Sciences Theory and Practice, 7*(1), 117–127.

Harmon, J. M., Wood, K. D., Hedrick, W. B., Vintinner, J., & Willeford, T. (2009, February). Interactive word walls: More than just reading the writing on the walls. *Journal of Adolescent & Adult Literacy, 52*(5), 398–408.

Himmele, P., & Himmele, W. (2009). *The language-rich classroom: A research-based framework for teaching English language learners*. Alexandria, VA: ASCD.

Himmele, P., & Himmele, W. (2011). *Total participation techniques: Making every student an active learner*. Alexandria, VA: ASCD.

Hoff, E. (2003, September). The specificity of environmental influence: Socioeconomic status affects early vocabulary development via maternal speech. *Child Development, 74*(5), 1368–1378.

Kelly, M. J. (2007). An organizational tool for all. *NEACT Journal. 16*(1), 14–17.

Kidd, D.C., & Castano, E. (2013, October 18). Reading literary fiction improves theory of mind. *Science 342*(6156), 377–380.

Kinchin, I. M. (2000). Concept mapping in biology. *Journal of Biological Education. 34*(2), 61–68.

Kramarski, B., & Mevarech, Z. R. (2003, Spring). Enhancing mathematical reasoning in the classroom: The effects of cooperative learning and metacognitive. *American Educational Research Journal, 40*(1), 281–310.

Krashen, S. (2004). *The power of reading: Insights from the research*. Portsmouth, NH: Heinemann.

Kuhn, D. (2000, October). Metacognitive development. *Current Directions in Psychological Science, 9*(5), 178–181.

Legare, C. (2012, January–February), Exploring explanation: Explaining inconsistent evidence informs exploratory, hypothesis-testing behavior in young children. *Child Development, 83*(1), 173–185.

Legare, C., Schepp, B., & Gelman, S. (2014). Examining explanatory biases in young children's biological reasoning. *Journal of Cognition and Development.*

Littleton, K., Wood, C., & Chera, P. (2006). Interactions with talking books: Phonological awareness affects boys' use of talking books. *Journal of Computer Assisted Learning, 22,* 382–390.

Martin, D. J. (1994). Concept mapping as an aid to lesson planning: A longitudinal study. *Journal of Elementary Science Education. 6*(2), 11–30.

Marzano, R. J., & Kendall, J. S. (2007). *The new taxonomy of educational objectives.* Thousand Oaks, CA: Sage.

Marzano, R. J. Pickering, D., & McTighe, J. (1993). *Assessing student outcomes: Performance assessment using the dimensions of learning model.* Alexandria, VA: ASCD.

McKenna, M. C., Conradi, K., Lawrence, C., Jang, B. G., & Mayer, J. P. (2012). Reading attitudes of middle school students: Results of a U.S. survey. *Reading Research Quarterly, 47*(3), 283–306.

Meehan, M. L. (1999). *Evaluation of the Monongalia County Schools' Even Start program child vocabulary outcomes.* Charleston, WV: AEL.

Miri, B., David, B., & Uri, Z. (2007, January). Purposely teaching for the promotion of higher-order thinking skills: A case of critical thinking. *Research in Science Education, 37*(4), 353–369.

Murphy, J. (2003). *Across America on an emigrant train.* New York: Clarion Books.

Nagy, W. E., Herman, P. A., & Anderson, R. C. (1985). Learning words from context, *Reading Research Quarterly*, *20*(2), 233–253.

Nagy, W., & Townsend, D. (2012). Words as tools: Learning academic vocabulary as language acquisition. *Reading Research Quarterly, 47*(1), 91–108.

National Endowments for the Arts. (2007). *To read or not to read: A question of national consequence* (research report No. 47). Retrieved from http://www.nea.gov/research/toread.pdf

National Center for Education Statistics. (2012). *The nation's report card: Vocabulary results from the 2009 and 2011 NAEP reading assessments.* Washington, D.C.: Institute of Education Sciences, U.S. Department of Education.

Novak, J. D. & Gowin, D. B. (1984). *Learning how to learn.* New York: Cambridge University Press.

Patten, K. B., & Craig, D. V. (2007, June). Ipods and English language learners: A great combination. *Teacher Librarian, 34*(5), 40–44.

Preus, B. (2012). Authentic instruction for 21st century learning: Higher order thinking in an inclusive school. *American Secondary Education, 40*(3), 59–79.

Roberts, M. Y., & Kaiser, A. P. (2011, August). The effectiveness of parent-implemented language interventions: A meta-analysis. *American Journal of Speech-Language Pathology, 20*(3), 180–199.

Roberts, T. (2008). Home storybook reading in primary or second language with preschool children: Evidence of equal effectiveness for second language vocabulary acquisition. *Reading Research Quarterly, 43*(2), 103–130.

Rodriguez, E. T., & Tamis-LeMonda, C. S. (2011, July–August). Trajectories of the home learning environment across the first 5 years: Associations with children's vocabulary and literacy skills at prekindergarten. *Child Development, 82*(4), 1058–1075.

Ruston, H. P., & Schwanenflugel, P. J. (2010 July) Effects of a conversation intervention on the expressive vocabulary development of prekindergarten children. *Language, Speech & Hearing Services in Schools, 41*(3), 303–313.

Sénéchal, M., & Cornell, E. H. (1993). Vocabulary acquisition through shared reading experiences. *Reading Research Quarterly, 28*(4), 360–374.

Sénéchal, M., & LeFevre, J. A. (2002). Parental involvement in the development of children's reading skill: A five year longitudinal study. *Child Development, 73*(2), 445–460.

Sharif, I., Ozuah, P. O., Dinkevich, E. I., & Mulvihill, M. (2003). Impact of a brief literacy intervention on urban preschoolers. *Early Childhood Education Journal, 30*(3), 177–180.

Shany, M. T., & Biemiller, A. (1995). Assisted reading practice: Effects on performance for poor readers in grades 3 and 4. *Reading Research Quarterly, 30*(3), 382–395.

Shany, M., & Biemiller, A. (2010). Individual differences in reading comprehension gains from assisted reading practice: Pre-existing conditions, vocabulary acquisition, and amounts of practice. *Reading and Writing: An Interdisciplinary Journal, 23*(9), 1071–1083.

Stanovich, K. E. (1986). Matthew effects in reading: Some consequences of individual differences in the acquisition of literacy. *Reading Research Quarterly, 21*(4), 360–407.

Starr, M. L., & Krajcik, J. S. (1990). Concept maps as a heuristic for science curriculum development: Toward improvement in process and product. *Journal of Research in Science Teaching 27*(10), 987–1000.

Stice, C. F., & Alvarez, M. C. (1987, December). Hierarchical concept mapping in the early grades. *Childhood Education*. pp. 86–96.

Stewart, T. L. (2008). *The Mysterious Benedict Society and the perilous journey*. Megan Tingley Books. New York: Little, Brown.

Swanson, C. B. (2009). *Perspectives on a population: English-language Leaners in American schools*. Bethesda, MD: Educational Projects in Education Research Center.

Tolkien, J.R.R. (2007, first published in 1954). *The fellowship of the ring*. London: HarperCollins.

Toscana, D. (2013, March 5). The country that stopped reading. *New York Times*. http://www.nytimes.com/2013/03/06/opinion/the-country-that-stopped-reading.html

Trelease, J. (1992). *Hey listen to this: Stories to read aloud*. New York: Pengin Books.

Viola, H. J. (1998). *Why we remember: United States history*. Menlo Park, CA.: Addison-Wesley.

Weizman, Z. O., & Snow, C. E. (2001, March), Lexical input as related to children's vocabulary acquisition: Effects of sophisticated exposure. *Developmental Psychology, 37*(2), 265–281.

Wiggins, G., & McTighe, J. (2005). *Understanding by design* (expanded 2nd edition). Alexandria, VA: ASCD.

Xu from Xianshan *Encouraging the traveler* (wood carving on wall at Angel Island). http://www.kqed.org/w/pacificlink/history/angelisland/poetry/three.html

Zohar, Dori, (2003). Higher-order thinking skills and low-achieving students: are they mutually exclusive? *The Journal of the Learning Sciences, 12*(2), 145–181.

Zusak, M. (2007). *The book thief*. New York: Alfred A. Knopf.

Index

Note: Page references followed by an italicized *f* indicate information contained in figures.

About the Authors

Dr. Pérsida Himmele is an Associate Professor at Millersville University in southeastern Pennsylvania. She has served as an elementary and middle school teacher, a district administrator, an English language learner program consultant, and a public speaker on issues related to student engagement and teaching in diverse classrooms. She has lived, taught, and studied in New York, California, and Pennsylvania, becoming actively involved in advocating for the passage of educational policies and funding formulas for the betterment of urban schools and English language learners. She earned her Ph.D. in Intercultural Education from Biola University and her master's in Elementary and Bilingual Education from SUNY–Buffalo. In addition to several articles, she and her husband, William, are the authors of the ASCD bestseller *Total Participation Techniques: Making Every Student an Active Learner* and *The Language-Rich Classroom: A Research-Based Framework for Teaching English Language Learners*. She'd be happy to hear from you and can be reached at languagerich@gmail.com or by phone at (717) 871-5770.

Dr. William Himmele is an Associate Professor at Millersville University in southeastern Pennsylvania. He has served as an ESL teacher and a speech pathologist, a higher education administrator, an international consultant, and a speaker on issues related to increasing student engagement and teaching English language learners. He served as the coordinator for the graduate ESL teacher certification program at Millersville University and has been an educational program consultant for several schools in various countries seeking to improve their school programs. He has lived, taught, and studied in New York, California, and Pennsylvania. He earned his Ph.D. in Intercultural Education and his master's in Teaching English to Speakers of Other Languages (TESOL) from Biola University. He and his wife, Pérsida, are the authors of several articles and the ASCD bestselling book, *Total Participation Techniques: Making Every Student an Active Learner,* as well as the ASCD book, *The Language-Rich Classroom: A Research-Based Framework for Teaching English Language Learners.* He'd be happy to hear from you and can be reached at languagerich@gmail.com or by phone at (717) 872-3125.

Keely Potter is a National Board Certified Teacher who currently teaches Language Arts to 5th through 8th graders at Dodson Branch School in Jackson County, Tennessee. Half of her time is spent in the role of "Master Teacher," which allows her to work with teachers in an instructional coach setting. Prior to teaching in her current rural district, Keely was a teacher, a literacy coach, and a reading specialist. She has also served as a professional developer and as a literacy consultant—which she continues to do. Most of her 21 years of teaching experiences have been in an urban setting, where we observed her weaving the same literary magic that she now currently performs in a rural setting. She was a contributor to Pérsida and Bill's previous ASCD book *Total Participation Techniques: Making Every Student an Active Learner* and served as a major contributor and as an instrumental consultant on this project. As such, her "stamp" can be felt throughout this book and we are so thankful for that. Her passions lie in supporting a culture of inquiry in teachers' learning communities and in encouraging all students to see themselves as lifelong writers, who lose themselves and find themselves in the act of writing. Keely would be happy to hear from you and can be reached at keelypotter@me.com